I0479948

Entrepreneurs Master Plan

— ---

50 Insider Business Startup Tips

continue to make books and other content like this. Thank you for the support.

Book production assistance by Digimasterz.net

Table of Contents

Purpose of the book

The goal of "Ultimate Entrepreneur's Blueprint" is to equip aspiring and current business owners with the insider information and expertise they need to thrive. This book is a valuable resource since it covers all the bases necessary for launching and maintaining a profitable company. Creating a business strategy and researching the industry are only the beginning; the book also intends to guide the reader through the steps of registering the business and opening an account for the company.

The book also discusses how to lay the groundwork for your company by doing things like creating a memorable brand, using social media, and giving stellar service to your customers. Marketing and sales techniques, working with staff and vendors, centering on the client, and making the most of available resources are all covered. Learning from mistakes, inspiring new ideas, and cultivating honest dialogue are also themes throughout the book.

This book is meant to provide the reader useful information that can be used right away in their own company. Its goal is to provide the reader with the knowledge and tools necessary to set up shop and keep it operating well, despite the inevitable challenges that will inevitably arise. The reader will be prepared to fulfill their business objectives and establish a healthy, profitable organization with the help of the advice and expertise presented in this book.

Introduction

Starting a Business is often a thrilling and demanding adventure. While there is no shortage of helpful materials for business owners, wading through it all may be a daunting task. This is why it's crucial to have access to insider information, such as the kind of tactics and techniques that can only be gained via actual work experience. No matter where you are in your business journey, this book will give you the essential things you need to know to succeed.

Everything from doing market research, business planning and writing a business strategy to establishing a solid brand identity and expanding your network is covered in detail in this comprehensive guide. You will acquire the skills necessary to analyze your pricing methods, make necessary adjustments, and maintain clean books and records. You'll also learn the value of cultivating meaningful connections with others, both within and beyond the company. You will also discover how to enhance and expand your firm on an ongoing basis, as well as how to make use of cutting-edge solutions to expedite operations.

If you want to know what it takes to make it in business, read this book. This book is a great resource for anybody at any stage of their company journey, from just getting started to expanding to the next level. If you want to succeed in business, you'll get the insider information you need from this book.

Those interested in beginning a company or expanding an existing one will find helpful information in this book. If you're an ambitious leader, entrepreneur, or small business owner, you'll find a lot to learn from this book. No matter where you are in your business path, you will discover helpful hints and advice here.

In sum, launching a company is an ordeal that calls for a lot of time, energy, and expertise. This book presents a thorough roadmap for realizing your dreams and equipping yourself for success. Thus, this book is essential reading for everyone who aspires to succeed in business, whether they are just starting out or are trying to expand.

I.   Insider knowledge & Tools Required

The process of launching a new company is difficult and complicated, requiring a broad set of expertise. You can increase your chances of success and learn how to deal with the various challenges you'll encounter if you have access to insider information. The term "insider knowledge" is often used to describe certain types of information and insights that are not publicly available yet may have a major influence on your company. This information may be gleaned from a variety of places, such as one's own experience, professional contacts, the experiences of corporate leaders, and scholarly studies.

Having insider knowledge is crucial for launching a company for a number of reasons:

- Decisions, such as picking a target market, naming your company, and creating a marketing plan, are all enhanced by firsthand experience and insight gained from insider knowledge. Using this data, you can make sure your firm gets off to a good start and avoids common pitfalls.

- Gaining an insider's perspective on the industry's trends, consumers, and marketing techniques will give you an advantage over the competition. With this knowledge, you can set your company apart from the competition and strengthen its position in the market.

- Getting access to insider information may help you save time and effort while running your firm. Methods for better managing staff and vendors, as well as advice on making the most of online marketing tools and automation software, may all fall into this category.

- It may assist in making better financial choices and preparing for expansion. Included in this is advice on selecting the best pricing plan for your firm, acquiring the necessary licenses and permissions, and opening a business bank account.

Success in business often depends on having access to confidential information. It may help you be more efficient and productive, as well as more competitive and successful financially. The information in this book will give you a leg up on the competition and improve your chances of creating a successful company.

Cost effective Tools and Products Required for Entrepreneurs

1. AmazonBasics is a collection of affordable and practical office necessities sold by Amazon, including as Paper Shredder, desks, seats, and lights.
2. The Amazon Kindle is an e-reader that provides mobile access to a library of books, periodicals, and documents for busy business people.
3. Amazon Echo Show is a Display screen with Alexa and a 13 megapixel camera in high definition. The 8-inch high-definition (HD) touchscreen, adaptive color, and dual speakers that Alexa offers help bring media to life. Use the 13 megapixel auto-framing camera to make

crystal-clear video calls. Use a revolutionary camera that frames and positions itself automatically during video conversations so you never miss a meeting. Just tell Alexa to call someone.

4. Laptops and tablets from Amazon's latest range are cost-effective and dependable business tools.

5. Cloud Cam is a security device for organizations, allowing owners to keep an eye on things from afar.

6. For businesses looking to back up and store data offsite, Amazon offers a series of <u>SSD hard drives</u>.

II. The Basics

A. Developing a business plan

No matter if you're just starting out or an established business looking to grow, creating a <u>business plan</u> is critical. Crafting a business plan requires dedication and hard work, but the reward is worth the effort. It requires considerable time, research, and consideration to get all of the pertinent details together. An organized, comprehensive plan includes following things, so that your objectives can be reached more easily.

Executive Summary

The executive summary is the first part of your plan that investors, lenders or potential partners will see. It's your opportunity to make a lasting impression and convince them that investing in your business is worthwhile.

Company Description

The company description is one of the main components readers of your business plan will encounter. Here, you can provide details about your company's history, management team and legal structure. A well-crafted company description can make you stand out from competitors and give potential customers a good sense of your brand.

Market Analysis

A market analysis is an integral component of any successful business plan. It demonstrates to lenders and investors that you've done your due diligence and can confidently confirm there is a niche for your product or service in a particular marketplace.

Your market analysis should provide an overview of the industry, a description of your target market and an assessment of competitors. Furthermore, it should include details regarding pricing and forecasting.

Management and Organization

The management and organization section of a business plan is essential for any document. It outlines your company structure, team members (such as owners, managers, and professional partners), and any financing arrangements you have in place. An organizational flowchart should clearly illustrate the chain of command, roles and responsibilities for your business. Furthermore, it should introduce each individual - their background and qualifications for their specific positions.

Managers must prioritize the efficient use of resources to reach their objectives. This involves creating a monthly budget to maintain cash flow and efficiently allocating finances between different projects and operations.

Products and Services

A successful business plan should clearly outline the products and services provided by a company. Whether you're selling physical items or intangible ones, this section helps potential investors comprehend your company's offerings and the value they provide.

The distinctions between goods and services are subtle, and depend on factors like tangibility, perishability, variability, and heterogeneity. Therefore, selecting the ideal product mix is critical for any company's success.

Customer Segmentation

Customer segmentation is a strategy used for identifying and targeting groups of potential and existing customers. Businesses can use it to increase sales, develop new product lines, and develop more effective customer retention tactics. The initial step in the process is to generate hypotheses about what separates different customers into segments. These may include demographics, geographics, psychographics and behavioral tendencies.

Marketing Plan

A marketing plan lays out the specific tactics and campaigns your business will use to promote and sell its products or services. It also provides a timeline for these activities to take place. The initial step in crafting a marketing plan is to clearly state your company's mission, vision and values. Doing this helps frame everything else within the document in context and makes it simpler for readers to comprehend.

The next step in developing a marketing plan is conducting market research and analysis. This helps determine how large your target market is and its potential for expansion. It also allows you to compare your business with competitors and pinpoint where you have an edge.

Logistics and Operations

Logistics refers to the process by which goods and services move from production or delivery to consumption. This encompasses transportation, distribution, inventory management and more. Logistics is a critical aspect of running any successful business, whether you're in retail, wholesale or manufacturing. A well-crafted logistics plan will increase your chances of success and keep your enterprise moving forward.

B. Target market identification

When developing a marketing strategy, it's important to first identify your target market so that you can narrow down on the specific kind of consumers you'll be trying to reach. The concept is that the company has a better chance of success if it targets its marketing efforts towards the people most likely to become customers and then adjusts its marketing mix accordingly, rather than trying to appeal to everyone in the market.

Five P's of your marketing mix

- Goods (what you're selling)
- Value (how much you're charging)
- Location (where you're selling)
- Advertising (how you're conveying the advantages of the product)
- People (who you're talking with)

Target Market Identification and Its Process

Your product or service may have wide appeal, but not everyone will really desire or need it. And it's a waste of time and resources to aim your marketing at the market as a whole, rather than at the consumer market, the industrial market, or the reseller market. To expand your customer base and boost sales, you may use a targeted marketing strategy that involves narrowing your emphasis from the whole market to just one specific subset.

To select your target market, you need to first determine who your ideal customers are, then divide the market into submarkets with similar needs and wants, and then zero-in on the most manageable and lucrative submarkets as the focus of your marketing efforts.

Suppose, for argument's sake, that you own a high-end men's formalwear boutique in your town. Your target demographic isn't the whole consumer market or even all men. Instead, you may target high-income males in a 60-mile radius, between the ages of 25 and 50, who crave status, by segmenting the market based on geographic, demographic, and psychographic criteria. If you know which guys are more likely to be interested in or in need of your goods, you can tailor your marketing strategy accordingly.

Mass marketing (which is aimed at a wide range of customers) and product-variety marketing (where a company consciously sets out to provide a wide selection of items to extend the client base) are two more examples of marketing methods. However, firms are gradually shifting from mass marketing to targeted marketing because of the latter's more potent marketing mix.

The Value of Identifying Your Target Market

Knowledge about your target market allows you to better design your product, pricing, and distribution methods to fit their requirements and wants, resulting in a more successful marketing mix.

It aids in the selection of effective promotional methods:

With a certain demographic in mind, it's possible to advertise your goods and services on the most effective channels, whether that's a specific social media site or a specific section of town.

Makes better use of scarce resources such as time and money:

Instead of spending time and money advertising to everyone, you may focus on the individuals who are most likely to be interested in what you have to offer.

Increases revenue and success:

Sales volume and profit margin may both increase as a result of the aforementioned variables expanding your marketing mix's visibility and accessibility.

Target Market Identification Methods

Review the features of the product or service: To better sell your product or service, write down a list of its qualities and advantages. If a laundry detergent uses a color-safe stain-removal formula, the result will be clean clothing that doesn't lose its vivid hue.

Find the selling points that will bring in customers: Find the one thing that sets your product or service apart from the competition among the characteristics and advantages you highlighted.

Figure out which aspects of segmentation are most important: Think about the criteria by which you'd want to divide the whole market into more manageable niches. Do this by compiling a list of the primary segmentation bases and determining which are most important to your target audience.

- Geographic (customers are targeted locally, statewide, regionally, or nationally)
- demographic (customers are targeted based on age, gender, race, income, education level, etc.)

- psychographic (identification based on attitudes, beliefs, emotions, lifestyle, and hobbies)
- behavioral segmentation are the major bases for market segmentation (identification based on various patterns such as purchasing occasion and loyalty status)

You should divide the market up into subgroups based on certain factors. The target market may be broken down into a few distinct subsets, which must be determined. A store selling both men's and women's footwear may elect to divide their customer base into subsets based on demographic factors such as gender and psychographic factors like interests, such as the frequency with which each subset engages in certain activities.

Select the most fruitful subsets of the market to focus on: Consider the financial resources of your company, the profitability of each recognised market segment, the market share held by your rivals, and the established position of your company in the market to determine whether or not it is profitable to pursue each identified market segment. Marketers may choose to zero-in on a certain subset of their target market for a variety of reasons, including a lack of resources, a lack of return on investment, a saturated market, or an attempt to enter a new market.

In short, in the marketing mix, a company can only concentrate on a certain subset of its potential clients, therefore identifying that subset is an important step. Discovering the motivations behind your consumers' purchases, segmenting the market according to demographics and other factors, and selecting the most lucrative subset of that market to focus on is what market segmentation is all about. Because of this, you may expand your reach and increase your income with a more optimal marketing strategy.

C. Choosing a business name

Choosing a name for your company is a crucial step in launching a successful venture. The name of your company will be the first impression you make on potential clients, so it's important to give some thought to it. A company's name should be one that stands out, is simple to say, and is straightforward to spell. It has to stand out from the crowd and avoid being confusing or maybe illegally identical to existing company names.

A comprehensive check should be done to confirm that the desired business name is not in use and is not too similar to other registered company names. You may do this by looking through various databases, such as those containing trademark information, government documents, and internet directories. If the desired company name is free, it should be registered as soon as feasible.

It's possible that you'll need to do more than just register the name of your company with the appropriate authorities before you can open for business in certain places. A tax ID, sales tax permit, business license, and any other necessary permissions and licenses for your line of work are all examples of this. Before opening for business, it's crucial to find out what kinds of licenses and permits are needed and how to go about getting them.

Business owners who invest in selecting a catchy and unique name for their venture and in securing the required licenses and permissions may rest certain that their business will be operating within the law and in full compliance with industry standards from day one.

In order to aid you in selecting a suitable company name, I have provided the following suggestions:

- Use a straightforward and easily-remembered approach. Customers will have an easier time remembering and relocating your business if you choose with a name that is simple to spell and pronounce.
- Think about who you're writing for. Choose a name that reflects the company's mission and image and will resonate with its target audience.
- Put your own spin on it. Select a name that stands out but isn't too similar to other companies' names to avoid any

possible misunderstanding or legal difficulties.

- Include relevant keywords. If you want consumers to quickly grasp what it is that you sell, a catchy yet descriptive name is essential.

- Think about the outcomes you want to achieve with your company. Pick a name that conveys your company's mission and values and that you'll be proud to use for years to come.

To avoid confusion with other businesses, it's important to make sure your potential company name isn't currently in use and isn't too similar to existing names in your industry. Consider asking for input on possible names from members of your inner circle as well as objective, outside sources.

Using these guidelines, you may choose a company name that will serve your needs while also being easily recognised.

D. Registering the business and obtaining licenses and permits

Starting a business legally requires registering your company and acquiring the required licenses and permissions. You may be certain that your company is functioning lawfully and in accordance with all applicable state, regional, and federal laws by following these procedures:

When starting a business in most countries, the first step is to decide on a legal structure for the company. Numerous structures may be used, the most common of which are the sole proprietorship, collaboration, limited liability company (LLC), corporation, and the non-profit. It's crucial to weigh the benefits and drawbacks of each structure carefully before making a final choice.

After deciding on a business structure, the following step is to register your company with the appropriate authorities. Paying any applicable fees and submitting articles of incorporation are usual first steps in this process. The specific actions and prerequisites will be unique to your company and its area.

Gather your company's EIN: The Internal Revenue Service (IRS) will issue your company a special identification number known as an EIN for tax reasons. One needs an EIN if they know or anticipate having workers. Get the appropriate licenses and permissions in order to lawfully run your company, which may vary depending on your industry and area. Permits for operating a company, for public health, and for protecting the environment are all examples.

It is crucial to investigate the unique standards for your sector since they may differ based on the kind of the company you are running. Tax registration is required in addition to establishing your company and acquiring an EIN. Among them are state income tax, unemployment insurance tax, and municipal sales tax registration.

In conclusion, getting the necessary licenses and permissions and registering your firm are critical steps in launching a profitable venture. It's a great way to keep your company on the up-and-up with the law enforcement and other authorities who oversee its operations. Do your homework to learn the rules that apply to your firm in its unique area, and then implement those changes.

E. Setting up a separate business bank account

Opening a company bank account is a fundamental step in running a successful enterprise, as it serves as a physical separation between the proprietor's personal and corporate funds. When opening a company bank account, it's important to keep in mind the following details:

- Identify the best financial institution: When deciding which bank to open a business account with, it's important to weigh the options in terms of proximity, costs, services, and reputation.
- Collect all necessary paperwork: An Employer Identification Number (EIN)

and other documentation of your company's legitimacy may be requested when opening a business bank account.

- Choose an account type: There are several options available for business banking, including checking, savings, and merchant services accounts. Think about the appropriate business bank account for your company.

- Many banks now provide online banking services, making it a simple and inexpensive method to handle your company's financial transactions.

- Set up a line of credit to ensure your company has access to finances in the event of unforeseen circumstances, such as a large cost or a drop in sales.
- Maintain precise records: Keeping precise records of all business bank account activities can help you maintain tabs on your spending and ensure that you always have cash on hand.

By following these guidelines and taking into consideration the specifics of your business, you may open a bank account for your company that will facilitate smooth financial management and the expansion of your operations.

III. Building a Strong Foundation

A. Establishing a strong brand identity

Brand identity is what makes your business memorable and unique. It reflects in your logo, marketing materials and how you communicate with your audience. To develop a unique and memorable brand identity, it's important to research your audience, value proposition and competition. This will give you an idea of what makes your business stand out and why people should buy from you instead of your competitors.

Research

The best way to develop a unique & memorable brand identity is to take the time to research your audience. By understanding their specific needs, pain points and aspirations you will be able to craft a more effective value proposition that can generate more engagement and sales.

When it comes to the best value proposition you can't really go wrong with something that focuses on delivering a solution to a problem that your target market is looking for. It's also important to make sure that your value proposition is a solid one that can stand up to the competition and win you new business. The key is to find the most relevant information and distill it into a single sentence that grabs and maintains your customer's attention.

Design

Brand identity is a combination of visual, content and tone choices. It also includes a logo and the voice of the brand. Once you understand your target market and the competition, you can start designing a brand identity. But don't forget that you need to make sure the design and the message are clear.

You'll also want to design a logo that will stand out from the crowd and be remembered for all the right reasons. There are many free logo design resources out there, but we'd recommend a professional service. This will ensure that you don't end up with a design that's not recognizable, or one that doesn't look good on your company's website or in social media posts.

Be Consistent

Your brand identity should speak to your audience in a way that speaks to their values and aspirations. It should also make them feel like they are part of a community that shares those values. The best brand identities stand for something, whether it's saving the environment or creating clothes that fit every body shape. These values give them a voice that resonates with their target market, and they build a lasting bond between the brand and its audience.

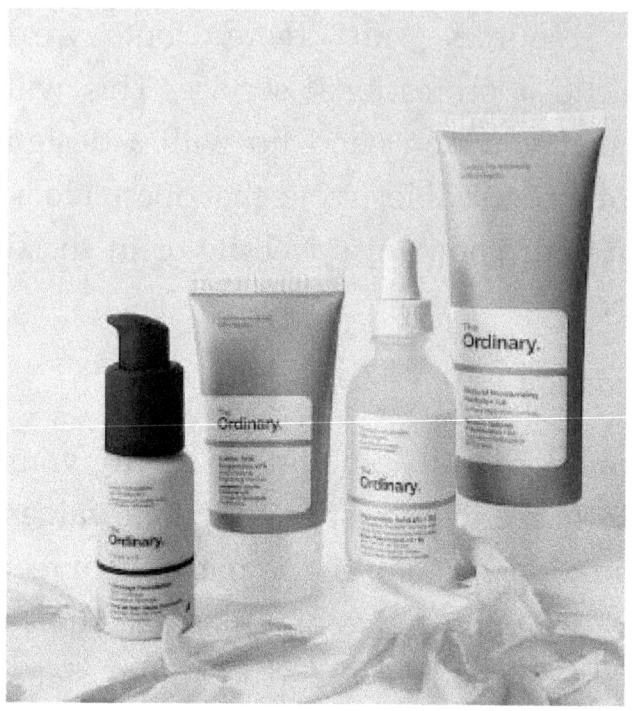

These brands plant seeds of customer loyalty, which helps them beat out their competition in the long run. But, to do this, they need to keep a consistent brand identity across social media and on their website.

Monitor

Once you've created a brand identity that appeals to your audience, it's important to keep it consistent. That means ensuring that your logos, color palettes, fonts, icons and other visual assets all adhere to your brand's mission statement and guidelines. This includes things like your brand voice strategy, email marketing specifications and packaging designs.

To keep your brand identity thriving, you need to constantly monitor its performance. This can be done through surveys, comments, social media discussions and more. This allows you to see what's working and what needs improvement. Then, you can implement the changes needed to maintain your brand's strength and credibility. It's a never-ending process, but it's essential to maintaining the success of your brand. The more you know about your target market, the easier it will be to create a brand identity that resonates with them and delivers on your business goals.

B. Utilizing social media

No matter your experience level with social media, it's essential to use it effectively in order to build a solid business foundation. A sound strategy can attract customers, solicit feedback and foster loyalty with existing ones. Furthermore, it may expand your market reach internationally as well.

Attract Customers

Social media can help draw customers to your business by showcasing your expertise and cultivating relationships. It also enables you to offer real-time customer service while improving the perception of your brand. People rely on reviews when making purchasing decisions, and a positive review from a satisfied customer can boost trust in your brand. Whether you share it publicly on social media accounts or embed it into your website, sharing customer appreciation helps cultivate loyalty among current and potential clients alike.

Another effective way to attract customers is user-generated content (UGC). These can be photos, videos or other artwork created by your shoppers and posted on your social media pages with their consent.

Get Customer Feedback

Receiving feedback is a crucial element of any business. Not only does it help you build a loyal customer base, but also provides an opportunity for improvement. When done effectively, customer insights can be a tremendous source of competitive advantage that directly affects your company's customer experience. Combining quantitative and qualitative methods will scale with your organization and provide the fastest path to real customer insights.

Feedback is also an effective way to demonstrate to your customers that you value their opinion and experience. Furthermore, feedback helps foster a culture of empathy within your organization.

Build Customer Loyalty

In today's competitive business environment, brand loyalty is paramount for business success. It encourages word-of-mouth promotion and conversions while requiring businesses to spend less money on customer acquisition. Social media is an invaluable resource for cultivating long-lasting relationships with your customers. It provides you with a platform to reach out and share your values with them.

To increase brand loyalty, focus on sharing content that encourages followers to feel connected and inspired by your company. This could range from captivating images and humorous posts or even videos that showcase your brand's distinct personality.

Increase Your Market Reach

Social media as a marketing tool is an effective way to solicit feedback from potential customers and cultivate existing ones. Popular platforms include Facebook, Instagram, Twitter, LinkedIn, Pinterest, YouTube and Snapchat.

However, some stand out from the rest. It is essential to select the appropriate social media platform for your requirements.

Do Market Research

Market research is an invaluable tool for gathering insight into your target market and customers, while helping you reduce marketing expenses. Before launching a new product or service, it is wise to conduct market research. Doing this gives you an edge over competitors and can help create a solid business foundation for the future.

Market research can be divided into two categories:

- Primary
- Secondary.

Primary research involves collecting firsthand information from your target market, eliminating the intermediary and guaranteeing that the data you obtain comes directly from those you wish to study.

Reduce Marketing Costs

Social media marketing is an economical way to generate leads and boost revenue. You can build customer networks on platforms like

Facebook, Twitter, LinkedIn, and Pinterest while advertising at no additional cost.

Social media offers businesses the unique advantage of being able to communicate with customers in real-time. Monitoring conversations and answering queries promptly can greatly enhance customer service experiences. When you promote your business on social media, be sure to direct followers to your website so they can complete actions or make purchases. This is especially crucial if you are selling products online.

Increase Revenue

Social media is an invaluable marketing tool that can increase sales for your business. Not only does it drive traffic to your site, but you can use social media to cultivate customer relationships and promote products you offer.

Facebook, Instagram and Twitter provide sophisticated messaging platforms that enable brands to engage directly with their followers. Furthermore, these services support visual content like short videos and photos.

C. Creating a professional website

If you want your company to succeed and make a name for itself online, you need a professional website. If you want to make a credible website, consider the following advice:

- Pick a domain that is both memorable and evocative of your company's identity.
- Spend money on a custom website design that communicates your brand's values and interests to your audience.
- If you want people to spend time on your website, it has to be user-friendly.
- Do not forget to include the fundamentals of your company, such as its services, goods, contact details, and guiding principles.
- Make sure that your website is compatible with all mobile devices.
- Use keywords, meta descriptions, and well-organized code to make your website more visible in search results.

- Make sure to constantly check and update your website with new information.
- Add in functionality like online chats and shopping carts if you plan on selling anything.
- Your website needs to be frequently checked for functionality issues and updated or fixed as needed.
- Think about the safety of your website and spend money on precautions to keep hackers out.

Your company's legitimacy, reputation, and ultimately its success all depend on how well-designed and maintained your website is. If you follow these guidelines, you should be able to build a website that does justice to your company and its offerings.

D. Networking with other business owners

If you want to expand your business, networking is an excellent starting point. But to make the most of this opportunity, make sure you network correctly. Networking is more than just speed dating; it's about cultivating relationships that can propel your business forward. Use these tips for successful networking with other business owners and you'll be well on your way to building an influential network!

Host Dinner Parties

Dinner parties offer the most intimate form of networking, providing you with a more personal and conversational atmosphere than at large events. Furthermore, it provides the chance to form new connections, especially with those whom you may not know well.

A host can have a major influence on a dinner party by creating an atmosphere of belonging and encouraging everyone to form connections. This requires having an attitude of generosity and the willingness to assist others.

Attend Local Group Meetups And Events

Networking with other business owners can be a great way to expand your reach and attract new clients. Additionally, it helps you cultivate an invaluable support system of people who can offer guidance and assistance when needed.

One of the best ways to achieve this is by participating in local group meetups and events. These groups usually feature members from various professions who can help you expand your network and increase your influence. To locate local networking groups near you, try conducting a Google search. Many organizations will have event calendars posted on their websites so that you can keep tabs on what's coming up.

Strategically Help Local Business Magnates

One of the greatest pleasures of networking is connecting with other like-minded individuals. This can be accomplished by attending local social events and getting acquainted with new acquaintances. Networking provides invaluable opportunities to learn about people's businesses and interests, making it a valuable asset for entrepreneurs. In addition to these social gatherings, consider joining some local groups and organizations as well. Doing so gives you access to knowledgeable people who can advise you on any potential pitfalls you may have missed before; helping avoid future mishaps and keeping you from getting left out in the cold.

Make Second-Degree Connections

Networking with other business owners is an invaluable opportunity to expand your network, but the secret to success lies in knowing how to do it correctly. There are various approaches you can use to achieve these objectives. One of the best ways to network with other business owners is through 2nd degree connections on LinkedIn. These are people directly linked to your first-degree connections on the platform.

Chat With Noncompetitive Peers

Networking with other business owners is an integral part of expanding your network and promoting your company. However, if the environment in which you work is filled with competitive individuals, it may prove challenging to form meaningful connections and exchange information.

When dealing with difficult people, the best approach is to remain patient and empathic. If you can't influence their actions, try offering something that helps them understand that you are not their adversary. To start, initiate by engaging them in conversation. Introduce yourself and explain your business venture, then ask them about theirs.

Host Meet And Greets For Local Entrepreneurs

Networking with other business owners is one of the best ways to stay abreast of industry developments and opportunities. Furthermore, it allows you to form connections within your region that can offer invaluable advice and resources specific to that region. When planning an event, factor in the time of day most business owners are likely to be in their offices. This will determine how long your meeting will last and help determine how efficiently it runs.

For small business owners, a meet and greet is an effective way to promote your company and reach potential customers and vendors. It can be an economical alternative to attending costly networking events.

E. Providing excellent customer service

Many companies owe a great deal of their prosperity to happy customers. For assistance, please consider the following criteria. Providing excellent service to consumers isn't a one-and-done deal; rather, it's a continual endeavor that spans the length of your company's connection with each individual client. Providing first-rate customer service should be seen as an investment rather than an expense.

Reliability

Customers are less inclined to purchase a product or use a service if they have doubts about its dependability. Customers are more likely to be satisfied with a reliable product or service, increasing the likelihood that they would use it again. The capacity to quickly and effectively address issues is another benefit of dependability.

In statistics, test-retest reliability measures how stable a metric is across time. This is often represented as a reliability coefficient, such as r. This is crucial for evaluating cognitive abilities, academic performance, and work output.

Assurance

Assurance is a crucial part of any service that aims to impress its customers. It entails keeping an eye on and analyzing a company's inner workings to make sure everything is functioning as it should and yielding the desired results. Feedback from customers, financial data, and staff evaluations are just a few examples of where assurance may be put to good use.

Moreover, the main goal of an assurance audit is to check the accuracy of a company's financial statements and identify any signs of fraud. Also, it's a great tool for making sure a company is being forthright and current with whatever data it shares. The financial information provided by assurance services helps businesses make informed choices and implement effective risk management strategies. They also provide an overarching perspective of the success and profitability of a company.

Tangibles

The quickest and easiest approach to win over loyal customers is to make them happier. Whether it means fixing problems promptly and accurately, responding to concerns with empathy, or just being generally kind to consumers, it will surely pay dividends.

The best organizations in this field are aware of, and dedicated to satisfying, their customers' wants and demands. This is crucial for generating client retention and referrals, which may provide returns as high as tenfold the original investment. The phrase "tangibles," which defines your actual buildings, equipment, and employees, is one of the most complex criteria. Having a well-maintained website or social media sites are also part of a professional image. It's important for every organization, regardless of its focus, to constantly improve.

Empathy

Excellent customer service relies heavily on the ability to empathize with the client's situation. Your company stands to lose consumers and reputation points if your customer service crew can't muster up any compassion for them. Your employees must constantly remember to show compassion for consumers, whether they are interacting with them over the phone, face-to-face, or in a chat environment. It's a fundamental human capacity that makes people feel seen, heard, and appreciated.

Feeling sad for another person or utilizing a feeling stopper (downplaying their feelings in order to boost your own) is not what empathy is about. It entails empathizing with another person's feelings and validating their viewpoint. The ability to empathize with another person entails not just understanding their feelings and actions, but also their internal mental processes. Empathy may be either cognitive, emotional, or physical.

IV. Marketing and Sales

A. Evaluating and adjusting pricing strategy

Maintaining profitability and competitiveness in the market requires a well-thought-out approach to pricing. When assessing and modifying a pricing plan, it is vital to take into account the following elements:

The manufacturing cost is an important aspect in determining the price policy. When setting a pricing, it's important to include manufacturing costs including materials, labor, and overhead. Examining the prices at which rivals sell comparable items is a crucial first step in developing a competitive pricing strategy. You may learn about pricing trends and the average purchase price of your target demographic this way.

Market segmentation: Knowing who will purchase your goods and how much they will pay can help you choose a fair pricing. What you charge for your product or service should reflect the value it provides to your target market. In order to set a fair price, it is important to take market demand into account. It is possible to charge more if there is more demand, and the opposite is also true.

Costs associated with marketing and public relations should also be factored in when setting prices. After giving these aspects some thought, you'll be in a better position to assess and modify your pricing approach as required. Keep an eye on market conditions and client feedback to adjust your price plan as appropriate. Keeping your firm at the forefront of its field and lucrative will be easier with this.

B. Staying organized and keeping accurate records

As a company owner, two of your most important responsibilities are to maintain your operations well-organized and your records in order. This will allow you to analyze profitability, prevent tax issues, and cultivate positive connections with both customers and suppliers.

You will be able to operate your company more efficiently and apply for loans with more confidence if you keep meticulous financial records. It's easy and quick to get started.

Effective Data Management

File organization is a good practice for anybody who uses a computer, whether for business or amusement. In addition, it is critical to regularly back up data in case of a computer failure or unintentional loss. The first step in effective data management is settling on the specifics of what data will be stored and how. If, for example, you need to keep sensitive company information, you'll want to use more advanced file organization methods than if the files only need to be accessible to you.

Keeping detailed records is critical to the development and profitability of any business. Not only can it help you avoid legal difficulties, but it will also help you maintain positive connections with your customers and suppliers.

Maintain financially independent profiles

Keeping your money in many accounts might make it easier to monitor your progress towards various goals. Create a different checking account for your vacation funds and a third for your home maintenance funds. When you have many different accounts, you can split up your spending and keep from making any costly mistakes. It's much easier to keep tabs on your spending and know at a glance how much of each designated fund is still available.

Keeping company and personal finances in separate accounts might simplify bookkeeping for a small business owner. It's a time saver come tax time, and it also helps investors and lenders get a more accurate picture of your financial health, which might increase your chances of getting a loan.

Get the Most Out of State-of-the-Art Digital Bookkeeping Tools

Spending money on cutting-edge cloud-based accounting software is time well spent. These applications streamline the process of company accounting by automating tasks such as the filing of receipts. Employees' time and effort spent on manual checks may be reduced with the use of such technologies.

For mobile entrepreneurs that spend a lot of time away from their offices, the best accounting solutions are ones that can be used from anywhere. This will guarantee that you are always on top of your books and ready to make payments, run reports, and create financial statements.

Classes in Corporate Management

There are a variety of tools available to help you keep organized and on top of your records, whether you're just getting started or already have a full-fledged business. Using a good application for managing a company is one option.

Earning a degree in business management will need you to take classes in everything from economics and finance to accounting and communications and even leadership. You will get a comprehensive understanding of business concepts in these courses and be better prepared to use what you study in the real world. It typically takes four years of full-time study to get a bachelor's degree in business management. You may be able to finish your degree faster by enrolling in an accelerated programme, but it's still crucial to choose your courses wisely and give some thought to your interests and abilities before making that decision.

Recurring Bills and Instantaneous Transactions

If you want your clients to pay their bills on time, every month, then sending them automated reminders is a great idea. In addition, they help customers avoid penalties for late payments and improve their financial planning.

Customers' payment records are analyzed to determine how often to send out payment reminders, which is a crucial feature of an automated system. The time savings and decreased effort for your agents is considerable thanks to this function.

To create recurring notifications for a certain group of customers, pick that group from the drop-down menu and go to the next step. Field, Operator, and Value allow you to set filters for this batch processing, so you may prepare for meetings based on things like customer type, open balance, and geographic region.

C. Investing in marketing and advertising

If you want to expand your business or attract new customers, creating an effective marketing and advertising strategy is critical. This guide will provide some key tactics you can utilize to reach those objectives.

Market development is a strategic initiative that assists companies in selling their existing products to new customers, increasing sales and profits. It may involve decreasing prices, launching an entirely new product or service, expanding distribution channels, or targeting competitors' customers.

Market Penetration Strategy

Market Penetration Strategy refers to the process of infiltrating an existing market (where products already exist) with a new product from your company or organization. It is generally viewed as one of the least risky business growth strategies. Crafting a market penetration strategy necessitates understanding your target audience and researching competitors' products, pricing strategies, and advertising campaigns. Doing this allows you to identify gaps in the market and craft tailored marketing initiatives to fill them.

Another essential step is calculating the average market penetration rate for your product. This measure helps you estimate market size and calculate total addressable market. Measurement is key when formulating your business strategy and creating an efficient operating model. An acceptable market penetration rate can make or break success for any venture, as it determines whether or not sales make a profit when sold to customers.

Market Development Strategy

No matter where your business is in its early stages or it is expanding rapidly, it is essential to always strive for ways to expand its reach and sales potential. This can be accomplished through various strategies.

One of the most successful growth strategies is market development, which involves introducing existing products to markets not already served by your firm or organization. To create a successful market development strategy, the initial step is to identify who would benefit from your product or solution. This requires conducting extensive market research that provides valuable insights about target audiences--their spending habits and other vital information.

Product Development Strategy

A product development strategy is the method companies use to design, test and release their products. It involves identifying a concept, getting market feedback about it, creating a prototype and crafting marketing and sales campaigns around it. Companies can utilize product development strategies to boost revenue by expanding into new markets. This could be accomplished through purchasing rights to sell another company's products or forming strategic partnerships to jointly develop and market a new item.

Businesses may utilize product development strategies to reposition existing items for different sales channels. This could involve raising a product's price or rebranding it in an appealing manner for consumers. Your strategy must be grounded in accurate research of your target market, competitors and consumer preferences. Doing this helps eliminate guesswork and conserves both time and resources.

Diversification Strategy

Diversifying your business can be a great way to maximize its growth potential and shield yourself from economic downturns. Companies can pursue diversification by expanding into new markets or adding products to existing ones. This may necessitate additional investment in marketing and advertising to publicize the new item or service.

For instance, a pottery shop could branch out into the mug market by providing more color choices. Doing so could attract customers who previously only bought one cup and encourage repeat visits and larger purchases. Companies often employ two primary diversification strategies - concentric and horizontal. Concentric diversification refers to launching new products that are closely related to other items already sold by the business, relies heavily on brand recognition and customer loyalty for transfer over to new offerings and operations, and relies heavily on outsourcing certain tasks.

D. Staying up to date on industry trends

Staying ahead of your industry requires being aware of the trends and shifts taking place. It's critical to pay attention and respond promptly when these shifts become major financial drains for your business. Signing up for industry newsletters is an effective way to stay informed. These publications, which are often free, are written by industry experts who can give you useful insight into current trends.

Sign up for industry newsletters

If you want to stay informed on industry developments, subscribe to an industry newsletter. These emails usually offer concise yet digestible summaries of recent information in your field. A well-crafted newsletter can help you cultivate a relationship with your readers, encouraging loyalty between both of you. Furthermore, it may serve as an excellent source for referrals.

When crafting your newsletter, ensure that you include a subscription form on every page of your website and in other places where potential customers can subscribe. Doing this will generate an email list with which you can gradually market with personalized messages in the future.

Read trade journals and magazines

Industry trends offer valuable information about your market and help you stay ahead of competitors. They may be caused by advances in technology or shifting consumer preferences. Staying abreast of industry developments requires reading publications pertinent to your business. These could include trade journals, trade magazines and industry newsletters.

Trade magazines and journals typically publish articles written by industry professionals or journalists with expert knowledge of the topic. They advertise products and services tailored specifically for this sector, often featuring case studies which detail how a service solved an issue or educational articles that impart knowledge on certain skill sets.

Read blogs

Blogs are an excellent way to stay abreast of industry developments. Additionally, they help your website rank higher on search engines and attract more visitors. Business bloggers typically discuss topics related to daily operations of a business, such as marketing, sales, and technology.

They provide details about new products, upcoming events and trends. This helps businesses boost their profits and enhance their bottom lines. These blogs are written by experts with extensive expertise, offering advice on how to develop your business.

Tune in to social media

Social media is one of the best ways to stay ahead of industry developments. By following experts and industry leaders on Twitter, Instagram or LinkedIn, you can access up-to-date information without worrying about missing out due to time constraints. You could also follow a blog that releases an article nearly daily. Having access to regular insights can be invaluable when it comes to setting your objectives in terms of driving sales and increasing brand awareness on digital channels.

Successful social media marketing starts with understanding your audience. To do this, regularly engage in conversations with followers and observe what works and doesn't work for you.

Subscribe to Google Alerts

Google Alerts are a free resource that any individual or business can utilize to monitor their online presence. It's an invaluable way to stay abreast of industry developments, keyword trends, and brand mentions.

Google Alerts offer the great advantage of being able to direct notifications directly to an RSS feed or Google inbox (great for remote teams). Furthermore, you have control over which notifications should be combined into one digest email - ideal for those who enjoy reading multiple emails each day!

Google Alerts are an underutilized surveillance resource that can be invaluable for anyone.

E. Offering promotions and discounts

For eCommerce business owners, offers and discounts can be a great way to increase sales. However, they're not suitable for every company so it's essential to understand how to utilize them efficiently. One popular strategy is offering flash sales, which offer substantial price reductions for a limited period of time.

This creates an urgency among shoppers and encourages them to act quickly.

Offer posts on Google My Business

Google My Business gives businesses a range of ways to connect with their customers. Posts can include photos, videos, links, and call-to-action buttons for easy engagement.

Offer posts enable your business to promote special sales or offers. They must include a title and start/end dates/times. These posts can help attract local customers to your physical store location and also serve to boost local SEO rankings.

Free samples

Free samples are an effective way to promote sales and raise brand awareness. Furthermore, it helps consumers make an informed decision about whether or not to purchase the product.

According to Sun's study, in-store free samples can be an effective marketing strategy that may boost sales. However, it's essential to consider customer demographics and the extent to which this promotional technique works in specific markets.

Research reveals that customers are more likely to respond to free sample promotions if they are younger, female, or have high household incomes. Since many direct-to-consumer brands rely on repeat business, this factor should be taken into account.

Buy one get one free

If you're looking to increase sales and move inventory, offering buy one get one free deals is a great choice for both retailers and customers. These promotions have become increasingly popular over time due to their attractive benefits. This type of offer has the potential to boost sales and improve conversion rates. It can also be utilized in combination with other sales or discounts.

Prior to offering any deal of this nature, it's essential to identify your target customers and set a price point. Furthermore, setting an expiration date helps customers realize how limited the offer is and encourages them to act quickly.

Cashback promotions

Cashback promotions are a widely-used promotional strategy that helps boost sales without undervaluing the product. They can also be employed to foster brand loyalty and build customer bases.

To successfully reach your target audience, it's essential to first identify who you want to appeal to and then determine how best to engage them with your offer. Whether your aim is to attract new customers or re-engage existing ones, different tactics will need to be employed. Studies have demonstrated that cashback shoppers often repurchase their items when given the chance. This behavior could be explained by mental accounting, the tendency for people to keep track of multiple accounts in their mind.

Lifestyle discounts

Offer lifestyle discounts to certain groups of customers, such as employees, students and members of the local community. Doing so not only encourages them to return again but it may also motivate them to recommend your business to others.

You could also offer flash sales to promote your products and services. These promotions, usually lasting one day, can be an effective way to boost sales. At Lifestyle, you'll find amazing deals on all sorts of fashion items - from winter wear to ethnic wear and shoes to accessories. Additionally, you'll find home and furniture pieces as well as high-end cosmetics and jewelry.

Flash sales and discounts

Offering flash sales and discounts are an effective way to draw in new customers to your website. Not only do these increase brand visibility, they increase revenue, and attract social media shares as well.

These promotions often aim to spark impulse buying and spur customers into action.

Furthermore, they help clear out inventory that's not selling well or has been sitting on the shelf for too long.

Deals often offer discounts or vouchers for specific products and categories, making them a great way to attract new shoppers, especially if your target market is price-conscious.

V. Building Relationships

A. Surrounding yourself with a supportive network

Successful entrepreneurs know the value of "surrounding themselves with a supporting network." Having people that believe in you and are willing to help you out when you're in a jam is invaluable. This is particularly helpful in the early phases of a business's launch, when a lot of stress and uncertainty may be felt by all parties.

A network of support may consist of many different kinds of individuals and groups. People like these may be found in the form of friends, family, mentors, business advisers, and even professional groups. You may learn a lot about your industry and how to run a successful company by talking to people who have been there and done that.

Attending networking events and conferences may be a great opportunity to meet like-minded people and expand your support system. Meeting other company owners and entrepreneurs at these gatherings is a great way to network and pick up new ideas. Joining a trade group or business association in your area may open doors to networking opportunities, educational opportunities, and other resources that can aid in the development of your company.

Joining online groups and forums that are specific to your field or specialty is another great method to meet helpful people and expand your network. These groups allow business owners to meet one another, discuss common challenges, and learn from one another's successes and failures. You may meet other company owners and entrepreneurs who can provide helpful advice and feedback by networking with them on social media sites like LinkedIn and Twitter.

Having a group of people who have your back is crucial to your professional success. The best way to overcome adversity and accomplish what you set out to do is to surround yourself with people who "get it."

B. Hiring the right people

When it comes to hiring the ideal personnel, there are various approaches you can take. But there are a few things you should keep in mind when making your choice. Begin by clarifying what you desire. Next, identify which skills you possess and consider how the role may evolve over time. Finally, anticipate any potential changes to this role.

Define exactly what you want

Determining your goals and objectives is the initial step in finding the ideal people for the job. The best way to do that is by taking risks and letting yourself go a bit - having the right people at the right place at the right time can make all the difference. Here are a few tips and tricks to get you on track, starting with coffee, alcohol and some great books!

Think about what skills you need

Sometimes, the skillsets required aren't necessarily determined by educational attainment; rather, they're personal characteristics that make someone well-suited for a particular role. For instance, you might require someone with a strong work ethic. That means they are capable of completing various tasks quickly and efficiently without much supervision from their manager.

Another essential skill you should consider is adaptability. Today's workplaces are evolving quickly, so hiring someone who can quickly adapt to changes and new challenges is a great fit for many roles. Additionally, you should assess their receptivity to feedback. Employees who become defensive or hostile when receiving criticism can be disruptive to their colleagues and colleagues alike.

Partner with a good recruiter.

Hiring the right people is one of the most essential steps you can take to build a steadfast, successful organization. A seasoned recruiter will assist in finding candidates who best suit your culture and company objectives.

A reliable recruiter will listen intently to your challenges and offer an objective assessment of your abilities. Furthermore, they may point out potentially troublesome scenarios that you might not be aware of yourself. You need a partner with extensive expertise in your industry, location and job function. This will enable you to hire the ideal person for the right role and save you time in the long run.

Use social media

If you are searching for a job, social media can be an excellent tool to network and stay updated on current information. But be mindful: social media sites may contain mixed content.

According to a recent study by Sherry Turkle, people are increasingly using social media for sharing emotional content rather than authentic communication, potentially leading to negative reactions. It is essential to remember that successful social media networking requires creating meaningful connections with people who can assist you. Begin by compiling a list of everyone you know who can offer assistance. This may include former co-workers, friends from school or college, churchgoers, and people in your family or community.

Don't rush

Though it can be tempting to hire quickly, making hasty decisions can prove more costly in the long run. Hiring someone who is not a suitable addition to your team results in lost productivity and costly training expenses. One of the most common mistakes people make when hiring is making a hasty decision based on their impressions. This can lead to poor choices and an overly optimistic view of a candidate.

Aside from the financial costs, a bad hire can also negatively affect morale within your team. It could disrupt workflow and impact overall objectives. In some instances, changing duties may be necessary; however before discussing this with an employee, take the time to understand why this shift is necessary.

C. Creating a positive company culture

A positive company culture can have a tremendous effect on employee happiness, productivity and retention. Studies reveal that contented employees tend to be more productive, stay longer and experience lower turnover rates than their less satisfied peers.

A successful company culture must be founded upon core values that permeate every aspect of the organization. By recognizing and upholding those principles, you will foster trust with employees and customers alike.

Identify Your Organization's Core Values

When creating a positive company culture, it's essential to identify your organization's core values. This step is crucial as it sets the framework for creating an enduring and healthy workplace environment.

Establishing and adhering to a clear set of company values is paramount for building trust, setting clear expectations, and giving your employees a sense of value. Furthermore, having strong values helps attract talented personnel who share these beliefs. Once you've identified your core values, be sure to review them frequently. Doing so keeps them fresh and at the forefront of everyone's mind.

Ultimately, your values should be unalterable guidelines that guide all of your business operations. Doing this allows your company to remain at a high level even when leadership changes, circumstances alter, or the team itself grows and matures.

Establish Trust

Building trust is one of the most essential abilities you can develop as an employee, manager or leader. It makes others feel safe relying on you, assured in your abilities and eager to collaborate with you.

Building trust in the workplace can be a difficult task and often necessitates altering your behavior. But in the long run, it pays off because it leads to a more productive working atmosphere. Establishing trust requires demonstrating your organization's values through communication and consistent action. This can be accomplished through various tactics, such as being clear and persistent in communicating your plans, as well as fulfilling commitments made.

Establishing a positive company culture that fosters open communication and vulnerability is essential. When these elements are present, people feel free to voice their ideas and take risks for the benefit of the business.

Maintain Clear and Consistent Expectations

Establishing clear and consistent expectations is essential for creating a positive company culture. Without them, teams often disband and productivity, initiative, and teamwork suffer. A clear set of job expectations provides employees with a comprehensive understanding of their roles, responsibilities and performance objectives within the company. Furthermore, it helps managers communicate clearly and foster trust between them and their staff members.

Leaders should communicate their expectations at every opportunity, such as team meetings and events, one-on-one performance dialogues and coaching conversations. Furthermore, they must 'walk the talk' by demonstrating what this means in practice.

Ensure Your Employees Feel Valued

A positive company culture encourages collaboration, productivity and employee satisfaction. Furthermore, it builds long-term loyalty and reduces turnover rates.

Create a positive company culture by emphasizing what your employees value most: acknowledging their efforts, encouraging teamwork and helping them reach their career objectives. Managers in positive cultures tend to be kind and empathic toward their employees, helping them feel appreciated and valued. They understand their needs and provide assistance during trying times.

Supervisors should make it a habit of talking regularly with direct employees, cultivating an authentic connection. Listening carefully and taking note of their worries can make a world of difference in both their work performance and morale.

D. Continuously improving products or services

Business can always benefit from improvements. Whether it be the products or services you offer, your operational processes or employee workflows, continuous improvement is a strategy that should be in place.

One of the keys to consistently improving your business is discovering opportunities for process simplification and quality enhancements. This iterative approach ensures you make incremental improvements over time, leading to increased throughput.

Strategic Planning

Enhancing products or services requires an ongoing strategy and process. This plan must be embedded in an organizational culture of innovation, involving employees on the front lines.

This approach emphasizes incremental, repeating improvements that occur over time. This philosophy is commonly referred to as "continuous improvement" or "kaizen." This strategy involves team members identifying and implementing changes on a small scale. Afterward, they use data to assess whether their changes have had an impact and determine if they have achieved what they set out to accomplish.

This strategy can be implemented in many business areas and is particularly successful when applied to product development teams. By employing this approach, product development teams are able to incrementally enhance existing products' quality while keeping them current with customer demands.

Be Consistent

Constantly improving products or services is one of the best ways to boost profits, boost market value, and stay ahead of your competitors. By identifying opportunities to reduce waste and enhance production efficiency, you can gain a competitive edge that helps maintain your leadership position in the market.

Continuous improvement is the process of continuously reviewing and assessing current processes, products, and services to identify opportunities for improvement. It also involves eliminating errors, increasing efficiency, and increasing productivity. This strategy has been shown to be successful in increasing sales volume and profits as well as increasing customer satisfaction levels.

Money management

Checks are a form of payment used to transfer money between bank accounts. They're printed with personal identifying information like the payee's name and their bank contact info, along with features like the check number, amount in dollars, and date of payment. In certain circumstances, checks may bounce if there's insufficient funds in the payer's account to cover them.

Continuously refining products or services can help companies come up with creative ways to streamline processes and make them more efficient. Doing so saves companies time and money by eliminating waste such as defects and overproduction. Furthermore, it elevates the overall quality of a product or service and gives companies an edge over their competition. Other methods for continuous improvement include user or client feedback, running tests and experiments, and implementing internal process changes, among others.

E. Building a strong reputation

Maintaining a stellar reputation for Relationships requires time, dedication, and hard work - but the rewards can be immense.

One of the best ways to build your reputation is by sharing your resources and expertise. However, be mindful not to undermine others' expertise by doing so.

Virtual Meetings

Virtual meetings are frequently utilized by teams that don't always have physical access to each other. They allow for staying connected with global team members, collaborating on projects, or even recruiting new talent.

When hosting a successful virtual meeting, there are several key elements to take into account. First and foremost, ensure the meeting has an objective. Communicate this information ahead of time and be prepared to answer any outstanding questions from attendees.

Decide the etiquette that will be followed at your meeting. For instance, do you require everyone to mute their microphones when someone else speaks? A well-planned meeting will be smoother to manage and avoid deviating into unproductive discussions. Furthermore, it should be on track to meet its objectives by the end of the session.

Social Media

Social media platforms offer customers and brands an invaluable opportunity to engage and build trust. Furthermore, these networks enable you to monitor both positive and negative mentions about your brand so that you can respond appropriately when needed.

A strong social media presence can be a game changer for your business. Not only does it help you stand out from competitors, but it also drives traffic directly to your website and generates leads and sales through these platforms. Social media can also be an excellent platform to share your resources and expertise with other professionals. Doing so could position you as a thought leader in your field, giving yourself more credibility as an authority figure.

Consumers expect companies to respond promptly and positively to comments posted on social media platforms. Doing so not only helps retain current customers but also attracts new ones.

Share Your Resources

A strong reputation is earned through hard work, connections, talent, loyalty and support from others. If you can effectively communicate these elements to others, your expertise in your field will be widely acknowledged.

You can build your reputation as a thought leader within your community; by being an advocate and helping others succeed, you will stand out as someone who contributes to making your industry stronger and more competitive. By sharing your expertise, you are helping make things stronger for all in the industry.

Additionally, you can build your reputation by projecting a professional image across all aspects of your business and social media accounts. This includes abstaining from language that might cause offended people to feel insecure or inferior; especially if working with clients who may have mental health issues or are in relationships where the behavior may be damaging for themselves or their relationship.

Share Your Humanness

Building a solid reputation for your business takes careful planning, extensive research and an abundance of creativity. To reach that level of success, you need to be the first person who contacts customers and rivals alike. A well-thought out strategy will generate the most buzz about your brand and its offerings, opening up opportunities for further collaboration that will propel growth in your business. Fortunately, there are plenty of resources available that can assist with creating the brand that works best for both you and your team members. Do you really want to stand out in a crowd by competing with your competitors for awards and accolades? Instead of competing on price or product, consider ways that can enhance customer experience and differentiate yourself from them. This is an effective strategy for differentiating yourself from rivals while increasing profitability. Making this connection between customer engagement and sales will pay off in the long run, so if done correctly, can help build a solid reputation that will last through time.

VI. Growth and Adaptation

A. Being prepared to adapt and evolve

Business is in a perpetual state of flux, and the organizations who can adapt to these shifts in the market are the ones that will ultimately thrive.

Listed below are just a handful of the many reasons why it's crucial to be flexible and progressive:

The market is in a constant state of flux, necessitating nimbleness from firms if they are to maintain their position as industry leaders. The development of technology, for instance, has revolutionized people's habits in many areas, including commerce, communication, and even the workplace. Businesses who have been open to new technology and modifications to their operations have flourished, while those that have lagged behind have faltered.

Adapting to the changing needs of customers: In order to be competitive, businesses need to be able to meet the ever-changing expectations of their customers. Eco-friendly and long-lasting items, for instance, are becoming more and more in demand. Businesses who can provide such items are more likely to thrive, while those that can't have difficulties staying competitive.

Competition is constantly seeking for new and better ways to do things, so businesses must be ready to do the same if they want to survive. If a business is unable to create novel goods and services, it may struggle to maintain its market share and competitive edge.

The business world is always evolving, therefore successful businesses are those that are agile enough to seize new possibilities as they arise. The growth of e-commerce, for instance, has provided new channels through which firms may connect with consumers and sell their wares; those who recognise and exploit these trends have a better chance of achieving sustained success.

As such, how can companies be ready for this change?

Some essential approaches are outlined below:

Read relevant news items and go to industry events to stay abreast of market and industry changes. This will keep you abreast of developments and allow you to make well-informed choices about how to develop and adapt.

Keep an open mind: Consider other viewpoints and methods, and don't be afraid to test your limits. In doing so, you may anticipate and be more prepared for market and industry shifts. Tech is always evolving, so businesses need to be open to trying new things if they want to maintain a competitive edge. Examples include companies that successfully use technological solutions to boost efficiency and productivity.

Work with others: Share information and collaborate with other companies and professionals in your field to stay abreast of the latest developments and most effective strategies. You'll be ahead of the curve and ready for whatever the future brings if you do this.

Maintain a mindset of constant evaluation and enhancement of your company. Soliciting consumer input on a frequent basis is one method of keeping up with customers' ever-evolving wants and demands so that you may adapt your offerings properly.

In conclusion, being flexible and open to change is crucial for every entrepreneur. Companies that are able to adapt to new market and industry conditions more quickly than their competitors have a better chance of long-term success. Businesses may increase their chances of long-term success by keeping up with the latest developments in their industries, maintaining an open mind, accepting new technologies, working in tandem with others, and always looking for ways to become better.

B. Using technology to streamline operations

If you want to boost the efficiency of your business, technology can be a great asset. Not only does this improve quality and reduce costs, but technology also gives employees more freedom and flexibility - leading to improved morale among staff members.

Begin by auditing all your processes and making necessary modifications to improve them. Perform a value chain analysis, evaluate handoffs, and identify bottlenecks in order to identify these areas for improvement.

Go Paperless

One of the first steps you must take is assessing your paper-based workflow. Doing this will give you a comprehensive view of how paper is utilized and what can be done to enhance processes.

For larger organizations, it is essential to involve a team of employees in this assessment process as they will be familiar with your processes better than you are. Take the time to go through your filing system and identify which documents need to be kept, those that can be scanned, and those to discard. Not only will this save space in your office, but it also makes searching for important documents much simpler when you require them.

Next, create an office-wide environmental initiative that encourages employees to reduce their paper usage. This is a worthwhile cause that many employees can support and it will save you money on energy costs and recycling materials.

Make Use of the Cloud

Businesses can leverage cloud technology to streamline operations. From backing up data securely, to automating processes, the right tools will enable your team to work smarter and more efficiently.

For starters, the cloud provides remote access to files and applications stored on servers in a data center. This enables employees to access their work documents and emails from various devices without having to download them locally on each one.

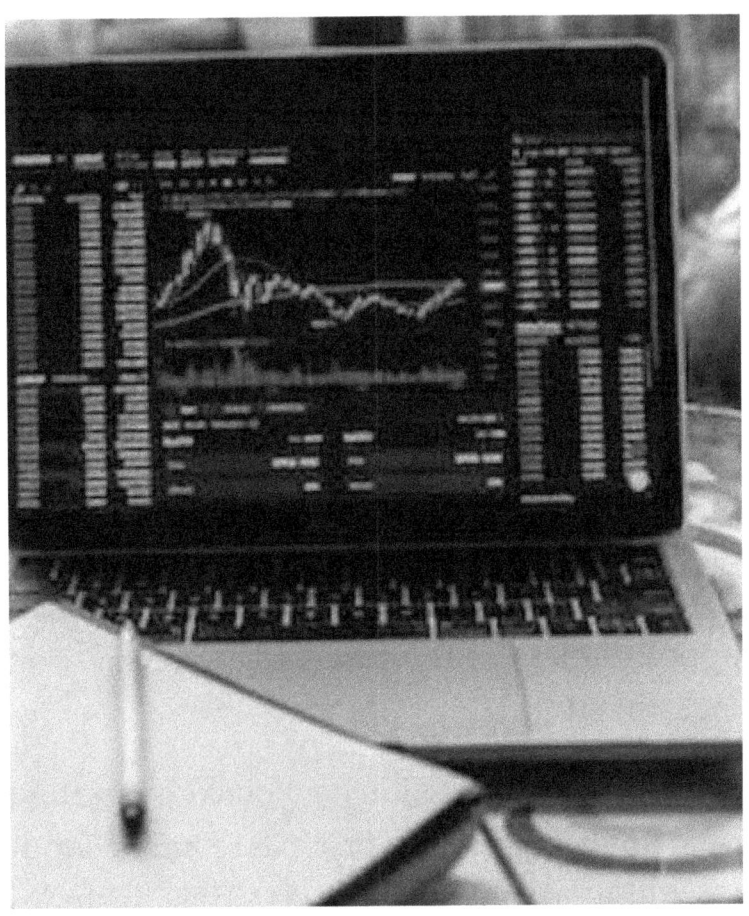

The cloud can offer companies greater agility when it comes to scaling their systems as they expand. For instance, if website traffic surges during tax season, the cloud infrastructure will automatically scale up to accommodate the surge.

Track Key Performance Indicators

Key performance indicators are an invaluable tool for organizations to monitor their progress. They give teams targets and milestones to strive towards, as well as valuable insights that will assist everyone in the business in making informed decisions.

Strategic KPIs measure performance over a longer time frame and focus on more critical areas of a company's operations. These indicators help executives detect trends and issues before they occur, as well as uncover opportunities to maximize return on investment.

Selecting the ideal KPIs for your organization is an ongoing endeavor that requires input from all parties involved. This includes informing employees about what these indicators are and how they can be utilized to enhance operations.

Improve Communication and Collaboration

Communication is one of the key elements for successful collaboration. This requires active listening, respecting others' opinions and encouraging active input. Technology can be an excellent tool for improving communication within your business. It enables teams to work more efficiently, share documents quickly and receive updates instantly.

Additionally, it can help you track key performance indicators, enhance people tracking, automate email and project management as well as manage maintenance invoices. But selecting the right technology for this purpose is paramount.

Automate Processes Wherever Possible

Technology can be an efficient means of cutting costs and increasing profits for your business. From automating customer service interactions to making it simpler for employees to locate files, process automation can have a positive effect on the bottom line of any organization. Select which processes you would like to automate and evaluate their value to your organization. Look for repetitive, rule-based or standardized tasks where auditing and logging are essential.

Take accounts receivable as an example; it is imperative that companies get their numbers correct every single time. Manually handling hundreds of invoices takes time and resources away from growth, increasing the chance for human errors or missed deadlines.

C. Offering payment options

Having a variety of payment methods available is essential to the success of any company, since this is what will ultimately convince clients to buy from you. Customers in the modern day have access to a wide variety of payment methods, and it is up to you to choose those that best suit your business's goals and those of your clientele.

The nature of your company should be among your first considerations when you design your payment system. If you operate an online shop, for instance, you'll need a mechanism for consumers to pay you electronically. However, if you have a physical storefront, you may need to settle for more conventional forms of payment like credit cards, debit cards, and cash.

Your intended clientele should also be taken into account. Customers have varying preferences when it comes to making purchases, therefore it's crucial to have a variety of payment methods. So, if your demographic consists mostly of millennials and Gen Zers, you may wish to accept digital payments like mobile wallets and internet banking. On the other hand, if you're hoping to attract a more mature clientele, it may be best to stick to tried-and-true options like credit cards and cash.

The fees and expenses of each payment method has to be thought about in addition to consumer preferences. Credit cards, for instance, are widely accepted, but they incur transaction fees that may pile up over time. PayPal and Stripe, on the other hand, may have reduced costs, but they also come with additional constraints, such as the types of businesses they allow and the countries they allow you to service.

Do some digging and check out the competition to find the finest payment methods to give your consumers. This may include investigating each option's security and trustworthiness, as well as any fees or costs that may be linked with its use. After deciding upon a suitable method of payment, it is essential to put it into place and give it a trial run to make sure it is functioning as expected. Implementing a payment gateway, connecting your bank account, and running through a few test payments can help guarantee a smooth and speedy checkout procedure for your consumers.

It is not enough to just provide clients with payment methods; they must also be informed of their alternatives. You may do this in a number of ways, such as by updating your website, putting instructions on receipts, and providing training for your staff.

Providing clients with a variety of payment choices is crucial to the success of any company, so it's necessary to find the ones that work best for you and your clientele. Providing safe, fast, and versatile payment alternatives is a certain way to make your consumers happy and encourage repeat business.

D. Maintaining a professional appearance

In the workplace, how you dress communicates a message about the value you put on your work. Taking pride in how you look at work demonstrates that you appreciate your employer and your position there. Clients, both new and old, may be more inclined to strike up a conversation with you during meetings and other professional events if you present yourself in a polished, businesslike manner.

It's worth noting that "professional appearance" is a vague term that may mean various things to different individuals depending on their occupation, company, and other factors. There are no laws that specifically protect against discrimination based on appearance, but all employers must follow standards for employment and not discriminate against federally protected classifications, such as race, religion or creed, and sex. Any company that has a dress code that excludes potential employees because of their hairdo, weight, or body piercings or tattoos should reconsider.

Style of business clothes

Jeans, T-shirts, shorts, sandals, and sneakers are examples of what people wear when they're in a casual atmosphere, such as when they're not at work. Dresses, blazers, blouses, sweaters, khakis, and button-down shirts are all examples of smart casual, which is another sort of casual wear with a sophisticated twist that is ideal for interviews in informal settings.

A business casual outfit might consist of a blazer, a skirt, pants, heels, or loafers, and is suited for interviews, client meetings, and many office situations. You should dress for success in formal business situations; which may include the use of suits, ties, and other fitted garments. Wearing dresses, skirts, blouses, slacks, pantsuits, and dark suits is appropriate for formal business meetings as well as award ceremonies and evening functions.

Advice on how to look your best at work:

Here are some points to keep in mind:

1. Maintain a tidy appearance

If you want to have plenty of time in the mornings to get ready for work, try waking up a little bit earlier. This way, you won't be rushed and can show up to work looking professional. One further way that eating breakfast at the table each morning might help you feel more alert and ready to take on the day is by boosting your metabolism.

2. Press your garments

It's a good idea to iron your clothing every day, either before bed or first thing in the morning, so that creases don't stand out. To keep your garments fur-free, you may wish to hang them up high enough that cats and dogs can't get to them. Employers and customers will appreciate that you take the effort to seem presentable and professional by wearing clean, wrinkle-free clothing.

3. Get ready for the next day's job by laying out your clothing the night before

If you spend too much time in the mornings sorting through your closet, you may find it helpful to choose and put out your clothing the night before. As a result, you won't have to hurry out the door in the morning, and you'll have plenty of time to get dressed in accordance with the dress code. If you get in the practice of laying out your clothing the night before, you may also start preparing your work schedule or food prep each evening, both of which will help you feel more prepared and organized during the day.

4. Take a look at the company's rules and dress code

For information on the appropriate attire for work at your company, peruse the employee handbook. Many businesses in the financial sector require their employees to dress in business casual clothes, whereas those in the technology sector tend to be more relaxed. When meeting with customers, many organizations want their staff to dress in a businesslike manner.

5. Examine your options for jewelry in advance

Put on your jewelry and practice walking out the door. If you wear jewelry to the office, try to choose pieces that are low-key and won't cause too much of a ruckus as you move about.

6. Keep in mind the days you will be interacting with customers

It's important to remember the days when customers aren't around if you're allowed to dress more informally at work. Whenever you're deciding what to wear in the morning or evening, go to your schedule and circle the days that you have appointments with clients. If you anticipate customers to show up unannounced, you may want to carry a change of clothing or a jacket to throw on.

7. Observe the attire of others around you

Consider what your coworkers wear on a daily basis for inspiration when deciding what to wear to work. Think about dressing like the rest of your workplace. If you want to go up the corporate ladder, take note of how your superiors and executives dress, and model your own wardrobe after that.

8. Prepare an outfit in advance of a meeting with a customer

If anyone on your team has ever met with this customer before, you should probably inquire if they have any idea what kind of attire is suitable. They may offer you a better sense of what to wear by describing the clothes they wore to the meeting.

Always wear business formal clothes if you are the first employee the customer has met. It is OK to wear a blazer over a nice blouse, button-down, or collared shirt. You may ditch the blazer in favor of something more casual if that's the vibe at work.

E. Investing in training and development

As workforces expand and change, employers must adapt to upskill and reskill their employees. Doing so can increase employee retention rates as well as boost morale. Investing in training and development for all employees at your company will not only make it a better place to work, but it will also equip employees with new skills that meet the demands of your business.

Attract High-Intellect Employees

Investing in training and development for Growth and Adaptation is an effective way to attract top-quality employees. Doing so will give your business a leg up over its competitors, guaranteeing you can stay abreast of new technologies.

Employees desire to feel valued and given opportunities for professional growth. To accomplish this goal, employers should offer a healthy work-life balance, comfortable office settings, and employee recognition programs. Furthermore, Millennials expect more from their employers than just health insurance and 401(k) contributions. To attract them, companies must provide benefits like gym memberships and flexible schedules.

Companies must ensure they attract the right talent. By considering seven areas job seekers evaluate when searching for jobs, enterprises can create strategies to draw in top candidates.

Increase Job Satisfaction Levels

Job satisfaction levels are an important factor for businesses that strive to retain their top talent and prevent turnover. Contented employees tend to be more productive and less likely to leave the company. A comprehensive training and development program is an efficient way to boost employee satisfaction and retain your top employees. This is because training provides employees with a clear path for their future advancement, giving them insight into what it takes to reach new heights.

A successful training program also rewards employees for the skills and knowledge they gain from their managers, increasing motivation to stay in a position and continue developing new abilities. According to LinkedIn Learning's "2020 Workplace Report," employees are more likely to participate in training when their efforts are acknowledged.

Keep Skills Competitive

Maintain your employees' skill sets by investing in training and development. Employees with the correct abilities will enjoy greater job satisfaction and morale, which ultimately results in increased productivity.

Upskilling and reskilling are essential elements in keeping your business competitive in today's rapidly-evolving marketplace. Industry demands, regulatory demands, and in-demand skill sets are constantly shifting, necessitating you to continuously retrain your workforce.

Companies investing in training programs typically experience improved sales and profits, as well as lower employee turnover and absenteeism rates. These benefits more than make up for the time and resources invested into employee education.

Better Retention Rates

Training and development is an excellent way to increase retention, as it allows employees to progress professionally and become more invested in their work. Furthermore, it gives them a greater sense of purpose and self-worth which may result in higher job satisfaction levels. High employee turnover rates can disrupt productivity, cause teams to stagnate and hinder diversity initiatives.

Retention rate should be measured as the percentage of employees who remain with an organization after a specified period. To calculate this figure, add up the number of employees at the start and end dates. The ideal retention rate is 100 percent, but this goal may not always be achievable. Oftentimes, it takes a significant investment in training and development to reach this mark.

Internal Promotion Opportunities

Instead of hiring externally, why not promote existing employees who possess the qualifications and expertise for a new role? This approach has several advantages: reduced cost, improved motivation and enhanced engagement.

Internal promotion is an efficient recruitment strategy for businesses seeking leadership-minded personnel with institutional knowledge. Additionally, it serves to retain top talent.

However, there may also be some drawbacks to consider:

Employees who are rejected for an internal promotion may experience disappointment and may even choose to leave the company altogether. It's essential to foster active communication between employees and management about training and development for Growth and Adaptation. This can be accomplished through regular all-hands meetings, company newsletters, Slack or Microsoft Teams channels.

VII. Building Strong Partnerships

A. Building relationships with suppliers

Establishing relationships with suppliers is an integral component of running a successful business. By cultivating positive supplier relations, you can guarantee your products and services are delivered on schedule with high quality standards. Begin by selecting suppliers who share your values. Doing so will make communicating with them much simpler and help create trust between both of you.

Choose suppliers that align with your values

Selecting suppliers who share your values is a critical step when building relationships with them. When your supplier shares your vision, it makes it easier for both of you to work together even during times of difficulty.

When selecting a supplier, inquire about their values and how they intend to incorporate them into the services they offer. If they can do this, it will be an indication of a mutually beneficial relationship between both of you. It is beneficial to get to know your suppliers personally. This involves spending time together, having conversations on the phone and scheduling face-to-face meetings whenever feasible.

Understand your suppliers' needs

Suppliers are essential to any business, so it's essential to cultivate strong connections with them. Having great suppliers helps your operation run more smoothly, provides superior service for customers, and boosts efficiency levels.

Maintaining a successful relationship with your suppliers requires effective communication, professionalism and some old-school good manners. It is also essential to keep communications open and honest, especially when dealing with those who are more important strategic partners for your business.

Be a great customer to your suppliers by always paying on time. Not only will this make them feel appreciated, but it will also strengthen the bond you share with them.

Be a great customer

Being an excellent customer is crucial in cultivating long-lasting relationships with suppliers. Your partners want to know that you value their contribution in your business and are doing your best to exceed expectations. Communicating clearly and concisely with them can help avoid misunderstands from arising, saving both you time and money!

Maintain regular communication with your suppliers, such as routine updates on product recalls and changes in pricing. You can do this via email, phone or meetings.

Maintain open communication

If you want to foster strong partnerships with suppliers, it is essential that you maintain open lines of communication. This requires sharing your plans, strategies and objectives.

Additionally, keep your supplier informed of any problems and help them determine how they can assist. Maintaining regular communication with your suppliers will make them feel like partners rather than just clients.

This approach will prevent misunderstandings and guarantee everyone is on the same page. This is especially pertinent when working with a supplier during times of supply chain volatility or disruption.

Give timely feedback

Working with a supplier you trust and value makes managing any issues that may arise much simpler. This is especially true if both parties are committed to open communication and honest feedback.

Due to its potentially destructive nature, a fractured relationship between your supplier and business can do more harm than good. Regular feedback allows your suppliers to identify performance issues quickly and take immediate steps towards improvement. It also conveys that you're committed to cultivating a long-term partnership.

Reward good service with loyalty

Customer loyalty programs are one of the best ways to reward your best customers. Not only that, but having a loyalty program can turn regular customers into brand ambassadors who spread awareness about your business.

Rewards can range from free products and discounts on purchases, to exclusive access to sales. They can be tailored according to a customer's buying habits and preferences. Some businesses even provide rewards that give back to their community, such as donating part of their reward points to charity. This is an effective way for businesses to connect with customers on a more personal level and appeal to their desire for ethical brands.

B. Staying informed about regulations

Staying abreast of regulations is essential for any business. Doing so helps companies stay ahead of emerging and evolving regulations, enabling them to meet the requirements of their governing bodies. Thankfully, there are a variety of useful tools to monitor regulatory changes. These include Google Alerts, Talkwalker Alerts, Mention, and Meltwater.

Google Alerts

Google Alerts is an invaluable notification service that keeps you up to date on regulatory developments. With it, you can set up notifications for specific keywords or phrases and receive emails whenever a mention of that phrase appears online.

Google Alerts is a free service, but there are some limitations. For instance, each user is only allowed 1,000 alerts. By doing this, you could potentially miss out on important updates from companies' websites and social accounts such as awards received, sales deals struck, and business expansion plans. Another limitation is the requirement to create a Google Account in order to use the service. This could prove inconvenient for those accustomed to Outlook, Yahoo or Proton email addresses.

Thankfully, there are other content-monitoring services to fill the void left by Google Alerts. Some of these tools also offer reporting and data visualization features which can be invaluable for brand reputation management as well as link building efforts.

Talkwalker Alerts

Maintaining compliance with regulatory changes is essential for all businesses, regardless of industry. Furthermore, staying informed can help build your reputation and generate links. One of the best ways to stay informed online about your brand is with Talkwalker Alerts. This free notification service can detect online mentions of your name, company, products or competitors and send them directly to you in a single relevant email.

Talkwalker Alerts is an excellent free alternative to Google Alerts and can be a beneficial tool for any company that wants to monitor online mentions of them. Setting it up is straightforward, and results are delivered in an RSS feed format that can easily be integrated into an existing RSS feed.

Mention(dot)com

If you want to stay abreast of all the recent regulatory shifts, Mention is the perfect service for you. This app monitors a wide variety of sources across the web including social media platforms, blogs, forums and review sites.

The great news is, you can customize your alerts according to your individual needs and priorities. Choose between daily summary alerts, weekly email digests or real-time push notifications for maximum convenience. If you want to know what people think about your brand, a monitoring app like this one is the ideal way to find out. Not only will you be able to view all of the recent buzz about your business but also have the chance to respond back. Doing so helps build an online reputation and ultimately grows your company. Plus, sharing these findings with team members keeps everyone up to date on online activity and how it's being managed.

Meltwater

Staying informed about regulatory updates is easy with a notification service. These alerts can be sent straight to your phone, giving you time to take action when something important arises. Meltwater is an ideal option, as it crawls review sites and alerts users when an issue arises. Plus, its customer support team is top-notch and the platform is simple to set up and utilize.

In fact, it is so good at recognizing issues that you can often learn about them before they become news stories, helping you save both time and money. Meltwater's unlimited keyword search capability lets you get to the bottom of things quickly and efficiently, making it the ideal tool for monitoring what people are saying about your brand online. Plus, with no limits on results pulled from 200 billion conversations - you won't miss a thing.

C. Offering benefits to attract and retain employees

Offering benefits to attract and retain employees is an integral component of any successful business strategy. These incentives encourage employees to remain healthy, productive, and loyal to your company. Employee wellness initiatives can range from smoking cessation and healthy eating programs, to exercise and stress reduction techniques. Furthermore, they promote employee engagement by taking into account individual needs and interests when designing the program.

Health Insurance

Health insurance is an employee benefit that pays for medical costs. It can be a great way to attract and retain staff members by giving them assurance that they'll receive the care necessary in case of an unexpected crisis.

Employers have the option to provide their employees with a range of healthcare insurance solutions, such as health stipends, health reimbursement accounts (HRAs), and group coverage through the Health Insurance Marketplace. To ensure everyone's needs and budget are met, employers should customize each employee's plan accordingly.

Dental and Vision Insurance

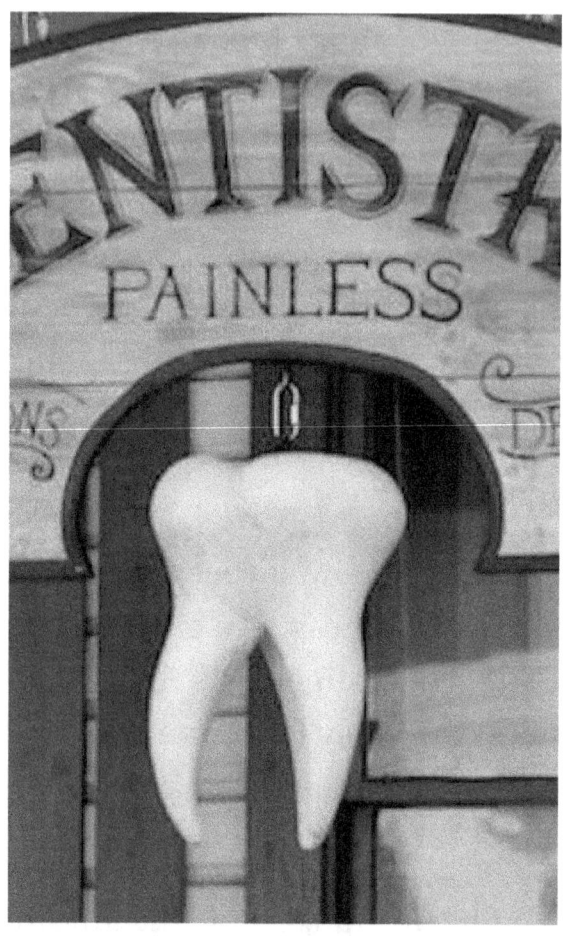

In today's competitive job market, offering employees quality benefits can be the difference between attracting and keeping top talent. One popular voluntary employee benefit that has become increasingly popular is dental and vision insurance. Dental and vision coverage can be purchased as a stand-alone policy or added onto health insurance plans. Oftentimes, these policies are purchased directly through the healthcare exchange or private insurers.

Retirement Benefits

Offering retirement benefits, such as a defined benefit plan, can be an effective way to attract and retain employees. These programs provide monthly payments to eligible employees upon retirement based on their salary and years of service with the employer.

Similar to health insurance, retirement benefits can have a positive effect on employee engagement and satisfaction. Unfortunately, an increasing number of Americans don't have access to retirement savings - an issue experts believe could negatively impact productivity as well as employee retention rates.

Vacation Time / Paid Time Off

Vacation time is one of the most valuable benefits for employees, whether it's used for travel or simply relaxing. Offering an accommodating paid time off policy can help you attract and retain staff in the long run. PTO (Personal Time Off) is an HRM policy that grants employees access to a pool of bankable hours for any purpose, such as sick leave, vacation and personal days.

Flexible Schedule

Offering flexible schedule benefits not only boosts employee morale, but it will also motivate staff to stay with your company for an extended period. This is especially helpful if employees have children or other personal matters that necessitate changing their work hours or schedules.

Flexible scheduling can assist your employees in reaching their educational objectives, and may even allow them to pursue a different career without leaving their current position. This helps reduce employee turnover and preserve valuable institutional knowledge from long-term employees.

Remote Work Options

Remote work options are an effective way to attract and retain employees. According to Owl Labs' State of Remote Work report, employees who have the option of remote work are 13% more likely to stay in their job than those without these advantages.

Implementing remote work options can be a challenging undertaking and necessitates an extensive multi-step process. Be sure to clearly communicate your remote work strategy and expectations to employees so they understand what's expected of them.

Wellness Benefits

Offering a wellness program to your employees is an effective way to attract and retain top talent. Employees want to work for an organization that values them as individuals, and this goal can be accomplished with the right wellness program.

Furthermore, healthy employees can save the company money on healthcare costs. This is because having healthy employees reduces their health risks and consequently decreases overall expenses for the business.

Education and Career Growth Opportunities

If you're searching to hire new talent or boost your retention rate, offering career growth opportunities is an effective strategy to attract and keep employees. According to LinkedIn research, 94% of employees say their employer would invest more in their professional development if it did so.

Education and career growth opportunities are especially significant to students, as they provide the first steps toward finding a job or career that matches their interests, abilities, and work values. Furthermore, having an effective educational and career plan can help students become more motivated and self-directed learners.

D. Collaborating with other businesses in the industry

Collaborating with other businesses in your industry is an excellent way to increase brand awareness and attract new customers. Additionally, it allows your business to grow and gain access to additional resources.

Collaboration can take many forms, from traditional alliances to networks of firms. It offers businesses of all sizes the opportunity to find creative solutions to their problems.

Cross-promotion

Cross-promotion is an effective way to raise brand awareness and generate leads on social media. It also allows you to repurpose your content across different channels, tailoring it for different audiences and communities.

Implementing a cross-promotion strategy necessitates selecting an experienced and trustworthy partner. Furthermore, knowing your objectives as well as the Key Performance Indicators (KPIs) you want to monitor are essential. One of the most successful cross-promotion strategies is working with other businesses in your industry. Furthermore, finding partners who share your core values can be extremely beneficial.

Interactive display

Collaboration with other businesses in your industry is one of the most efficient methods to promote your brand. Doing so demonstrates that both businesses have agreed on common objectives and values.

Collaboration through remote working can be especially advantageous for smaller companies that may not have the resources to hire someone full time to manage social media campaigns. It also gives your employees the ability to work remotely with someone in another location, leading to new ideas and products for your company.

Interactive displays are flat-panel monitors that enable users to interact with content displayed on screen. They have applications in retail & hospitality as well as education, with growth expected over the next ten years.

Influencers

Influencer marketing is the newest trend in marketing, offering businesses an effective way to build their brands. Influencers are online personalities who cultivate a large fan base through social media promotion of their work.

Influencers come in many shapes and sizes, so it's essential to find one that aligns with your objectives. For instance, if you're a travel brand, seek out bloggers or vloggers with an enthusiasm for traveling. These partnerships are an effective way to reach an audience with a high likelihood of purchasing your product or service. Furthermore, they create a positive connection with your brand that increases trust among consumers.

Guest Posting

Guest posting is an effective way to establish authority within your industry and acquire useful SEO backlinks. Google uses links as one of their primary criteria when ranking websites, so having quality backlinks from other sites can make a major impact on the success of your SEO campaign.

Once you've identified some potential sites to target, use a tool like Moz's Open Site Explorer to check their domain authority (DA). This can tell you if the website is trustworthy and will provide valuable value in terms of links and traffic if your guest post is published there.

Next, search for blogs that cover a similar topic as your own. They are likely more responsive than other readers since they already have an understanding of what you have to offer.

Podcast

Podcasting is an effective marketing tactic that can be utilized to reach new audiences, generate leads and build your brand. Additionally, podcasting helps establish yourself as an authority figure within your industry which may increase your perceived value and ultimately boost sales.

To start your own podcast, it is important to select a format that aligns with your goals and objectives. For instance, if you are an independent dfs hfss hacker or freelancer, starting a podcast that focuses on marketing advice could be beneficial. Once your show is created, edit and publish it onto a platform of your choosing. There are plenty of details to take into account so take your time and do it right the first time.

E. Attending trade shows and events

Attending trade shows and events is an excellent way to discover new business opportunities, as well as build your professional network. In 2021, businesses must work hard to build trust with customers. To do this, businesses must demonstrate their values online and through other stakeholders. Furthermore, they need the right personnel to convey these messages effectively.

Doing business – boosting sales

Trade shows and events offer many opportunities for companies looking to grow their sales, both short- and long-term. One of the most beneficial is setting up a kiosk or stall at one of these events where people can come in and learn more about your product offerings.

To maximize success in your industry, it is best to attend events that target core consumers and potential suppliers. The rewards are plentiful; one of the most notable being an influx of quality leads and prospects eager to do business with you.

Reaching new target groups and cooperation partners

Trade shows are an invaluable opportunity to network and make new business contacts face-to-face. Not only that, but they offer valuable opportunities to promote products or services, stay abreast of industry developments and gain insight into your competition.

Make sure your presence at a trade show is noticed by posting regular updates on social media sites throughout the event. This can be done by an assigned team member and will keep followers engaged while generating leads from your trade show marketing campaign.

When selecting which trade show to attend, be sure to select those that align with your business objectives and target market.

Research the event's past media coverage, prominent speakers, social media activity and anticipated attendance to find the ideal fit for you.

Showing presence

Trade shows offer brands an invaluable chance to connect with potential customers and deepen relationships with existing ones. But this can only be successful if the right steps are taken both prior and during the event. Investment in a well-designed booth and experienced staff are essential elements. These individuals must possess comprehensive knowledge about all aspects of the company and be able to engage prospects effectively.

Add some personality to the event by hiring a music band or DJ. This will keep the energy high and all attendees content.

Building trust

Trust is essential for your sales success. Today's buyers have many options and require your time and focus. Establish trust by demonstrating your competence. This doesn't need to be a scripted sales pitch; instead, ask questions, listen intently to their problems, and offer helpful suggestions.

Demonstrating that your company cares about them makes it much simpler to earn their trust and loyalty. Doing this allows you to expand your market share without needing additional customers or higher marketing expenses.

Retaining customers

Retaining customers is key for any business looking to sustain long-term growth. After all, it costs five times more to acquire a new customer than it does to keep an existing one, so this strategy is imperative for any successful venture.

Companies with large advertising budgets and a strong sales force may prioritize events that help them meet objectives such as closing sales, servicing accounts, or other customer-retention activities. Conversely, those whose marketing communications mix is effective at keeping existing customers but inefficient at identifying and selling new prospects may turn toward shows that are likely to draw in current clients.

Gaining market share

Trade shows and events are an effective way to uncover new business opportunities, as they provide attendees with the chance to form personal connections and boost brand awareness at once. Due to the COVID-19 pandemic, many businesses are considering whether attending such events is worth it.

Personal networking as a door opener

Attending trade shows and events is an ideal way to network with potential partners, new customers, or even just gain more business. Before going, make sure you have the right people in mind; for instance, if selling door openers is your target market then knowing what types of products are popular there would help you communicate better with those businesses and offer direct feedback on your own items which could ultimately improve them and boost sales.

VIII. Customer Focus

A. Offering quality guarantees and warranties

One of the best ways to increase consumer trust in a product is by providing quality assurance and warranties. This will give new customers peace of mind that they have nothing to lose by buying from you, which in turn helps convert site visitors into buyers.

Some guarantees are straightforward, such as a money back guarantee or 90-day trial period. On the other hand, some brands take things to the next level by offering lifetime guarantees. Although this may be seen as risky by some, it will help your brand project an enhanced image among consumers and foster trust in its products' quality.

Increase Consumer Confidence

Manufacturers, retailers or online e-commerce businesses need to instill consumer assurance in their products for improved customer engagement. Offering quality guarantees and warranties is an effective way to boost sales, foster trust with customers and establish a reputation for excellence.

Promoting your guarantees and warranties is essential for success. This should include signage, flyers, envelopes and other marketing materials. A guarantee is a written promise from the seller that, should their product fail to meet certain quality standards, they will repair or replace it free of charge. It also specifies the conditions under which they are responsible and which conditions are excluded.

Additionally, offering a product protection plan in addition to your warranty can be beneficial. Doing so helps guard you against dishonest buyers who purchase your item, use it for a short time, and then return it.

Leverage the Warranty to Close the Sale

Increase customer satisfaction by offering them a solution that works. One effective way to do this is offering an appealing warranty. A quality home warranty can help boost retention rates and boost profits simultaneously; offering free inspections or money back guarantees are just some of the options available. More involved services like home repair or appliance replacement might require more involved warranties too - in short: having one is essential for small business success!

Protect Your Reputation

Your company's reputation is an essential asset that attracts customers and retains talent. However, it also poses a potential risk. Even one negative incident can have detrimental effects on both of these areas; even minor slip ups could cripple both of these factors.

Offering quality guarantees and warranties for your products can be an effective way to build up your business' reputation. Not only does providing a warranty boost customer confidence, but it also makes them feel more secure about purchasing from you. No matter if you sell furniture, bicycles or cars, the quality of your product can influence customer loyalty to your brand. Offering a warranty that covers any repairs or replacements will increase your credibility in the eyes of buyers and increase brand loyalty.

Online reputation protection is an active strategy that creates controllable assets such as positive content that outranks negative search results on Google's first page. Doing this can shield your brand from being destroyed by viral news stories, competitor websites, or harsh customer reviews.

Build Customer Loyalty

By offering customers the option to return or exchange defective products, your business will be on the path toward cultivating customer loyalty and increasing profits. Offering these options helps boost existing customer lifetime value (CLV) and foster loyalty among new ones.

In addition to product warranties and guarantees, providing customers with excellent customer service is critical. A recent Harris Interactive survey revealed that 89% of respondents switched to a competitor due to poor service experiences. Customer loyalty is a journey that requires continuous improvement across various business functions. One effective way to measure customer retention is by tracking the percentage of customers who stay with your company for an extended period of time.

B. Developing partnerships with complementary businesses

One of the most important things you can do for your company's growth and expansion is to form relationships with other companies in your industry. This entails teaming up with companies that provide complementary goods and services. By combining services, you may better serve clients, expand your respective markets, and boost revenue for both companies.

In order to successfully form partnerships with firms that compliment your own, consider the following guidelines. Get specific with who you want to collaborate with: First, you should investigate the market and identify companies that provide complementary goods and services. In your search for partners, prioritize organizations that operate in a market and serve a customer base similar to your own.

Once you've zeroed down on some likely collaborators, it's time to start establishing some solid rapport with them. Get out there and meet other company owners and industry leaders at trade events and via direct contact. Incentives like joint promotions and discounted prices are also recommended.

First, it's crucial to establish your aims and objectives before beginning collaboration with a complimentary company. It's important to discuss your goals for the relationship and the amount of time, energy, and money each of you is prepared to put in so that you may reach those goals. Prompt and clear communication is the cornerstone of every successful cooperation. Keep in close communication with your spouse to ensure that you are on the same page at all times. Any problems or concerns should be dealt with quickly, and everyone involved should pitch in to find a resolution.

Do some cross-promotions with similar businesses; this will help you reach more people and raise awareness of both brands. Customers that buy both yours and your partner's items or services should be offered special offers or discounts. Cross-selling and client retention will both benefit from this.

It is crucial to give exceptional customer service while dealing with a complementary company. This includes resolving any concerns raised by customers in a timely manner and delivering solutions that are tailored to their specific requirements. It is crucial to constantly assess the state of your cooperation. Evaluate how the combined promotions have impacted your company and the level of pleasure your customers feel. You may use this information to determine whether to keep the partnership as-is, make adjustments, or dissolve it altogether.

In conclusion, building relationships with other companies that might benefit yours can help you expand your operations, raise awareness of your brand, and attract a larger customer base. As long as you keep these things in mind, you should have no trouble forming partnerships that help both of your businesses thrive. However, remember that partnerships demand investment of your time, energy, and resources; choose your partners carefully.

C. Using customer feedback to improve products or services

Utilizing customer feedback to enhance products or services is one of the most powerful and successful strategies to grow your business. It can result in dramatic improvements across all aspects of operations, from customer service processes to product offerings.

The secret to successful customer relations is listening and responding appropriately. Doing this allows you to cultivate a lasting connection with your clients and ensure they keep coming back for more.

Update your product or service

Making the most of customer feedback requires recording and saving it all. Doing this allows you to repurpose the comments, suggestions and compliments in a creative way - such as creating a new product feature or design with this information. Taking customer input seriously will keep them delighted and returning often.

To maximize customer insight, you should also create a strategy to make it easy for employees to provide feedback. This can be accomplished through an encouraging company culture that promotes employee interaction and collaboration. Doing this will lead to more informed decisions and an engaged workforce. The most efficient way to do this is by setting standards and procedures that can be adapted across all employee types.

Establish a clear policy for handling customer complaints and use an effective follow-up procedure to monitor and assess results. Doing this will give your employees something to strive towards and allow you to maximize their efforts.

Share social listening feedback internally

Social listening isn't just for marketing professionals -- everyone in your organization can gain from a better insight into customer perception of your brand. By sharing feedback with sales, product development, and higher-level management teams, you can help implement changes that increase customer satisfaction levels.

It is essential to link social listening with your business goals, such as increasing conversion rate or customer retention. Doing so will enable you to utilize insights for strategic success and meet those objectives.

For instance, if customers are talking about your dealership's experience, you can use this data to make improvements like increasing staffing or inventory levels. Doing so may improve customer satisfaction and boost sales at the same time.

Improve your employee training process

Employee training can help companies enhance employee performance and foster loyalty among staff members. It also gives employees insight into how their skills are being utilized, which may prove advantageous if they wish to advance within your organization.

Training programs allow your company to test a new performance management system and reinforce the importance of employees meeting goals. They may also increase employee engagement and productivity, which in turn benefits your bottom line. When reviewing your employee training process, ask for feedback from team members. This feedback can give you a comprehensive view of how things are going and where improvements need to be made.

Follow up and relay improvements to customers

One of the most critical actions you can take for your business is using customer feedback to enhance products or services. By following up and communicating changes back to customers, you'll create a strong bond that could result in increased loyalty, advocacy, and revenue.

Establishing a customer feedback loop is an effective way to do this, but it necessitates careful coordination across your entire organization. This includes collecting insights from customers, making sure they reach the correct people, and disseminating them widely so everyone can benefit from them.

For instance, if a customer sends you feedback about an issue with your website or links, you should reach out directly and show that you have taken note of their worries and that they are an integral part of the team. Furthermore, showing them how much value they add to the business can shape how others perceive your brand in the future. This step is vital since such feelings could potentially influence future purchasing decisions.

D. Focusing on your mission and values

If you're starting a business, one of the most essential steps is to focus on your mission and values. Doing this will help build an enduring foundation for your company and guarantee its success in the long run. Crafting an effective mission statement takes effort and time, but the rewards are worth all of the effort.

Do Keep It Short and Concise

When crafting a mission statement, it's essential to remain concise and precise. Lengthy prose rarely captures attention and can hinder communication between staff members and customers alike.

As you begin crafting your mission statement, consider the core values that define who you are as a company. These can range from quality and customer service to innovation and sustainability. Next, assess how your products or services align with those values. This is essential since your mission statement serves as a marketing tool and must resonate with your target audience.

Remember, your mission statement should be an accurate representation of your business and flexible enough to accommodate long-term objectives. Doing this allows for future expansion without restricting employees or customers in any way. The more effort you put into crafting the perfect mission statement, the greater its success at attracting and keeping customers.

Do Think Long-Term

Maintaining a long-term plan is essential for keeping your business on the right path. It helps you identify and address problems as they arise, giving you an indication of what success looks like. Furthermore, your goals can serve as inspiration when planning future expansions or selecting which type of financing works best for you.

Finally, it's essential to remember that while planning for the future can be beneficial for any business, ignoring what exists today could prove disastrous. That is why focussing on your mission and values is so crucial; not only will this help you avoid common errors made by business owners but also give your company a higher chance at long-term survival.

Doing the above may seem intimidating at first, but it's achievable. A plan will ensure you have everything necessary to launch and develop your company successfully. The key is making sure to incorporate the most crucial aspects of your mission into every decision you make so that you can meet all deadlines while staying within budget.

Do Find Out What Your Employees Think

Establishing a mission statement that you and your team can live by is the initial step in aligning with your business values and priorities. Doing this will enable you to prioritize tasks more effectively, while giving employees clear direction when making decisions.

Discovering your employees' opinions on a mission statement is another way to make it more effective and meaningful for your company. Get their input through focus groups, surveys, or one-on-one conversations.

Finally, the most effective way to maintain your mission statement is by communicating it clearly to employees when changes need to be made. Don't be afraid to get their input or implement changes promptly when desired. Doing this will create a strong company culture and attract top talent for your company; additionally, increasing productivity and making profits easier are also benefits that follow from such changes.

E. Being open to feedback and constructive criticism

One of the most beneficial skills you can develop is being open to feedback and constructive criticism. Establishing a work environment where feedback is valued encourages personal and professional growth by creating an encouraging atmosphere for others to express themselves.

But how do you determine if the criticism is valid? Often, our first instinct is to reject it as unfounded. But how do you decide whether your initial reaction should be positive or neutral?

Stop your first reaction

It is normal to feel overwhelmed when receiving negative feedback. However, you don't have to. Try your best to remain calm and avoid reacting at all!

Stopping your first reaction is the best way to prevent any knee-jerk reactions like defensiveness, anger or even pride. This allows you to evaluate criticism objectively and determine whether its points of view are valid or not. Remind yourself that feedback is an opportunity for growth and development. It can enhance your abilities, work product, and relationships while helping you meet the expectations your manager and others have of you.

Remember the benefits

Receiving feedback has many advantages, from improving work performance to building trust and forging relationships. In the long run, feedback will make you happier and more productive.

Given this, constructive criticism can be unsettling. Therefore, the best approach to handle feedback is to maintain a cool head and remember that it's an integral part of learning. Try to understand your criticizer's motivation and perspective, as they likely did their best to deliver constructive criticism. While this may not always be possible, it will help you get the most out of your next feedback exchange. To do this effectively, be a good listener and ask questions to deconstruct their feedback in an insightful manner.

Be a good listener

Listening is one of the most essential skills you can develop. It helps others feel valued, understood and heard. Good listeners understand that communication often doesn't manifest itself verbally; rather, it often manifests through body language and facial expressions. They strive to read these cues to decipher what someone else is feeling beneath the words spoken.

They allow the speaker to finish their thought without interjecting or asking questions that take away from what they're saying. They don't want to fill up the speaker's balloon with all of their things to say before the conversation comes to a conclusion.

Say thank you

Saying thank you is a key aspect of being open to feedback and constructive criticism. Not only does it demonstrate your integrity, but it also allows you to process the criticism fully and learn from it. Saying thanks is an expression of appreciation that we all understand, and it's an effective way to let someone know you value their help or assistance. Research has demonstrated the power of gratitude, with studies even finding it to increase our sense of social worth from day to day.

When receiving feedback from a friend or colleague, it is especially important to make an effort to thank them for their time and efforts. Not only will this boost your self-worth, but theirs as well!

Ask questions to deconstruct the feedback

If you receive constructive criticism, be sure to ask questions to deconstruct it and express your viewpoint. Doing this can help you comprehend what was said, which can serve as a great opportunity to refine your work product in the future. If someone remarks on your writing, for instance, that it "lacks clarity," you might ask them for specific examples and further explanation of what needs to be improved.

This will enable you to refine your work and prevent repeating the same errors in the future.

Furthermore, it's an effective way to build trust and foster stronger relationships with those you collaborate with.

IX. Utilizing Technology and Tools

A. Using social proof to build credibility

Social proof in the form of testimonials, reviews and trust icons is an effective way to foster credibility. It helps customers make an informed decision, feel secure about their choice and feel part of something bigger.

Selecting the type of social proof that best meets your needs can set off various emotional reactions. The most powerful forms include testimonials from current customers, experts and industry leaders.

Testimonials

Testimonials are one of the most influential ways to build credibility with potential customers. They provide them with a glimpse into how other people have used your product and how it has benefitted them.

They're an effective way to build trust, particularly amongst those who may not know if your product or service meets their needs. In addition to customer testimonials, you can also obtain endorsements from influential industry figures who use your products frequently. The ideal testimonials come from customers who have utilized your products or services and are willing to share their impression with others. They should also be relevant to your target demographic and buyer personas.

Effective testimonials will demonstrate that your product or service meets a consumer need and alleviates their pain point, encouraging prospects to convert.

Reviews

Reviews are an integral component of conversion-boosting pages and can be used to encourage potential customers to buy. Remarketing emails to those who added items to their basket but didn't complete the purchase can be a great way to use reviews as motivation, or share them on social media to motivate people towards purchasing.

Consumers rely on online reviews to research brands, products and services before making a purchase. Around half of consumers say they would travel further and spend more money with a business that had positive (and authentic) reviews.

Review platforms such as Google and Amazon are the two most common review platforms, although local search and directory sites are also popular. If collecting reviews on your ecommerce website, ensure the form looks and feels optimized so consumers can input their details accurately. Limiting pages required will help reduce reviews that get abandoned before completion; additionally, include floating labels to let customers know what information is required and what type should be typed in.

Trust Icons

When customers are ready to purchase from your website, they want assurance that you can fulfill your promises. The most effective way of providing this assurance is through social proof - testimonials, reviews and ratings from delighted customers. Positive reviews and ratings should be prominently displayed throughout your site, not only on the homepage but also product pages and checkout forms. Doing this builds trust among visitors who are much more likely to convert after seeing what you have to offer.

Another effective way to build credibility is with third-party endorsements and certification badges that demonstrate your brand's membership in reliable networks or organizations. For instance, being part of Microsoft's Partner Network can help strengthen your brand's credibility among tech-savvy prospects.

Case Studies

Case studies are an effective way to demonstrate the success of your business for customers. They're also an effective way to build credibility and position yourself as a thought leader within the industry.

Case study research is a type of qualitative inquiry that draws from several disciplines, such as sociology, anthropology and psychology. In this approach, researchers collect data from various sources such as interviews, protocol analysis, field studies and participant-observations. Researching primary sources can often provide researchers with detailed information about a particular phenomenon or situation. Furthermore, they may help identify important topics or themes that need further exploration.

Case studies can be beneficial when assessing new policy initiatives or service development, and in other ways to understand the effects of an event or phenomenon on a group of people. The key is selecting an appropriate case study that meets both your needs and research objectives.

B. Developing a system for tracking and responding to customer complaints

Establishing a system for tracking and responding to customer complaints can help you resolve issues promptly, improving customer satisfaction levels and ultimately increasing revenue. Customer complaint tracking applets allow teams to maintain a consistent complaints database with easily customizable forms with predefined fields. Furthermore, these applets can be accessed on a secure cloud platform for faster data access and analysis.

Status Platform

Establishing a system for tracking and responding to customer complaints is essential for creating a successful business model. Doing so can increase customer satisfaction and brand loyalty, especially when complaints are handled promptly. Complaint management software can be an invaluable asset for any business, no matter its size. Not only does it help you understand why customers are unhappy, but it also gives you valuable insights into how to enhance products or services.

The ideal complaint management software solutions provide an organized, straightforward method to monitor customer issues and requests. Furthermore, these systems offer company-wide visibility through a centralized portal for easy tracking across multiple locations.

A superior complaint tracking system will enable you to conveniently access and review conversation history and CRM data from other applications in one location, so that you can gain insight into what occurred before the issue was reported. Doing this makes it easier to comprehend the broader situation at hand and promptly address any problems that arise.

Live chat systems

Live chat systems offer a host of features to help you track and address customer complaints. These include an internal knowledge database, ticketing systems, integrations with CRM applications and other third-party applications.

Live chat software for customer support is an efficient way to enhance your sales and support operations. It quickens resolution times while decreasing customer effort - leading to greater satisfaction and loyalty from your clients. A successful live chat system should offer an intuitive user interface for both agents and consumers. Customers desire a smooth, continuous conversation experience that feels natural and comfortable.

Agents require access to the necessary data in order to respond promptly to customer questions. A great live chat system should integrate with your CRM, providing essential customer data in real-time so agents can provide a superior support experience.

Prices for these systems may vary, but most vendors provide starter packages with additional features and integration capabilities. These plans tend to be an affordable solution for small businesses and startups.

Trouble ticket programs

Establishing a system for tracking and responding to customer complaints is essential for maintaining customer satisfaction in your company. Additionally, this will give you insight into the underlying cause of any problem.

The ideal trouble ticket program will facilitate every step of the ticketing process, from customer submission to receiving feedback from agents who resolved it. Doing so, you can enhance your support team's work and offer customers a better experience. A reliable trouble ticket system will automatically analyze a customer's issue and assign it to the appropriate representative who can provide assistance. This saves time, while decreasing miscommunication between representatives and customers.

The ideal trouble ticket software should provide features that enable agents to work simultaneously on cases submitted from various support channels and set alerts for responses. It can also be linked with CRM software, so employees or customers can review relevant customer or employee information while working on a case.

Customer relationship management systems

Establishing a system for tracking and responding to customer complaints can help you better understand your customers' needs and offer them excellent service. Furthermore, it helps prevent you from losing even your most dedicated customers.

Customer relationship management (CRM) systems are software programs that integrate all aspects of a company's relationships with customers, from marketing and sales to customer service and other interaction processes. CRM systems are an invaluable asset for businesses of all sizes. Not only do they improve customer experiences and boost sales, but they can also streamline internal operations.

CRMs can be hosted either locally or in the cloud, depending on a company's requirements. On-premises systems require expensive hardware and IT resources for operation; furthermore, they are more vulnerable to downtime and upgrades.

C. Using analytics to measure marketing and sales success

Predicting and measuring marketing and sales success are critical components of any business plan. Without accurate analytics, companies may spend money and resources on strategies that don't yield results.

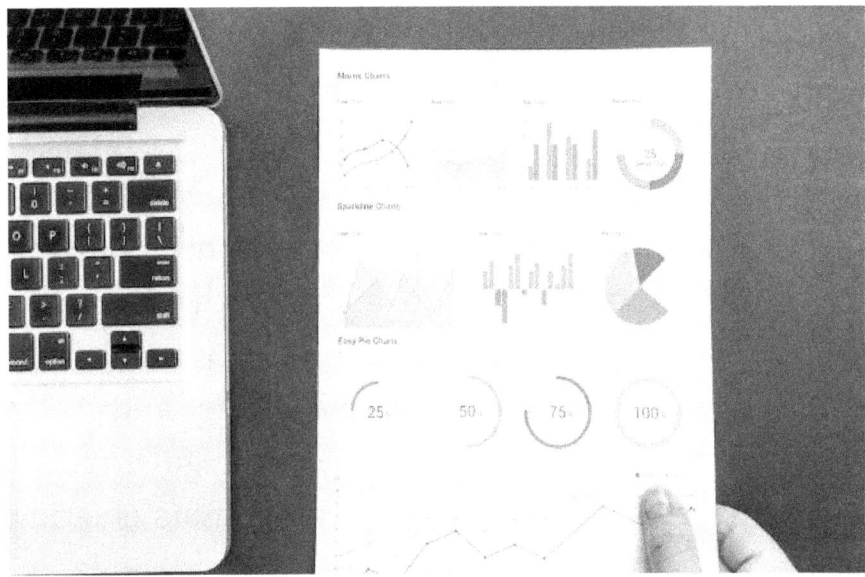

Data collected through analytics can give businesses a deeper comprehension of customer behavior and help them adjust their strategies accordingly, ultimately increasing their overall business productivity.

Predicting Sales

Predictive analytics enable businesses to forecast sales based on past sales, demographic trends and behavioral indicators. They can be employed independently or alongside traditional methods for improved forecast accuracy.

Predictions grounded in data can be invaluable when making crucial business decisions, from hiring and managing to budgeting and goal setting. They also enable you to identify issues before they escalate into larger issues, allowing for course correction and improved morale. Sales forecasting can also identify trends that could influence your marketing and sales strategy, such as changes in government policies or new industry competitors entering the market. They also assist you in understanding how seasonality may impact your sales volume.

Accurate sales forecasting is essential for your company's success. Not only does it help you identify potential issues for early resolution, boost the performance of your sales team, and make informed business decisions, but it can also identify opportunities to enhance the sales funnel and boost revenue.

Identifying Consumer Trends

Trends are an invaluable tool for monitoring industry shifts. By understanding trends, businesses can stay ahead of the competition and provide products and services tailored to their consumers' needs.

Trend analysis is a complex endeavor that necessitates business professionals to comprehend three essential components: basic human needs, change (both long-term shifts and short term triggers), and innovations. Perceiving where and how these come together to form new levels of customer expectation is essential for identifying points of tension between what people desire and what's available.

Consumer trends are driven by both long-term, macro changes and more immediate factors like specific technologies, political events, economic shocks or environmental incidents. These triggers play an integral role in shaping the nature and direction of trends; businesses must be able to recognize them before they become widely adopted.

Tracking industry and consumer trends can be a time-consuming endeavor, but it is achievable. Trend analysis methods such as keyword research, competitor analysis, and data analytics help businesses stay abreast of the most recent industry developments and consumer demands.

Optimizing Your Sales Funnel

A sales funnel is an integral element of any successful marketing and sales plan. It helps guide prospects from awareness to conversion, turning browsers into paying customers.

Businesses can optimize their sales funnel in several ways to boost conversion rate and maximize profitability. One effective method for doing this is using analytics to measure marketing and sales success. The initial step is to decide what data needs to be collected. This decision will depend on your overall business objectives and current growth stage.

Once you have the right data, it's essential to comprehend your customer journey so that you can tailor your sales funnel accordingly and offer them better service at each stage. The sales funnel consists of four stages -- Awareness, Interest, Desire and Purchase. Optimizing each stage can result in higher conversion rates and more customers.

Measuring Success

Measuring the success of your marketing strategy is an integral part of any business. It helps you allocate budget funds more efficiently and avoid investing in a strategy that does not generate profits. Analytical data can also assist in comprehending your audience, so that you may craft content that appeals to them and offer products and services they require. Doing this helps your business expand and remain competitive within its industry.

Predictive analytics utilizes a wide range of data to forecast trends, problems and solutions. These algorithms can project future consumer behaviors, employee productivity shifts and supply chain management issues.

Predictive analytics can tell you which products sell best during a promotional campaign or what customers are searching for online around certain holidays. They also help predict customer churn, prevent fraud and streamline manufacturing processes - but be sure to utilize this technology correctly in order to get the most out of it.

D. Staying up-to-date on latest technology and tools

Staying abreast of the most up-to-date technology and tools is essential for any business leader. Doing so gives you a competitive edge and accelerates your company's expansion. However, staying organized can be a real challenge. Thankfully, there are plenty of resources available to assist you!

Read Tech Blogs

In today's technology-driven world, it is essential to stay current on all of the newest tools and innovations. One way of doing so is through reading Tech Blogs.

Tech blogs are written by knowledgeable individuals with a passion for the subject matter. They aim to share their insight on the latest technology and tools while engaging with their audience in an approachable and conversational style.

Follow Tech Thought Leaders

Staying current on technology and tools requires following tech thought leaders on social media. These experts spark important conversations that spur creativity throughout the tech sector.

The tech industry moves quickly, with new innovations and technologies appearing daily. That means thought leadership content must be timely and pertinent in order to be effective.

High-quality Technology Thought Leadership content offers industry-specific answers and insights that share best practices without being a product pitch. It should also cover all stages of the buying journey, from early consideration through decision-making and implementation.

Sign Up for Tech Newsletters

Staying current with the newest technology and tools that can propel your business growth is essential for all small businesses. Whether you're in sales, executive or management roles, staying informed on industry innovations allows you to better comprehend what your team needs as well as that of potential customers.

Tech newsletters are an effective way to get your messages in front of relevant audiences. They provide carefully curated, succinct summaries that busy professionals like yourself can quickly scan. These newsletters often take a more relaxed approach to tech news, focusing on topics like culture, design and sustainability. As such, they make for great reading material for those seeking something lighter and more entertaining.

Join Tech Forums

Tech forums are an excellent platform to exchange news and information about new technology. Here you can read discussion topics related to computer hardware and software, get peer-to-peer advice, and access free tech support.

Business development executives are searching for ways to utilize emerging technology and tools to streamline sales processes and boost growth. These forums feature case studies from members who have successfully adopted these tech innovations in their businesses.

The tech industry is highly competitive, and companies are always searching for ways to stand out. Here, 12 members of Forbes Business Development Council discuss some of their top picks in technology and explain how it can help boost your business.

Attend Tech Events

Technology events offer an invaluable way to stay abreast of the newest tools and technologies, as well as provide networking opportunities with industry luminaries. Tech conferences are large-scale in-person gatherings that revolve around a single topic.

They often feature keynote speakers, sessions and workshops on the topic at hand.

Summits are another popular type of event in the tech industry. These gatherings typically tackle a specific issue and bring together experts from both sides of an argument to discuss it.

The conference industry is flourishing, yet it can be intimidating to navigate. There are various types of tech conferences available and which ones best suit your professional objectives will depend on which ones fit best.

Listen to Podcasts

Are you searching for ways to stay current on technology and tools? Podcasts are an ideal option. They can be downloaded onto computers, smart devices and many other platforms.

Popular tech podcasts such as The Joe Rogan Experience and Serial offer in-depth conversations with leading experts. Other shows specialize in specific topics, like TED Talks Daily.

Finding the ideal podcast for you requires searching using either your listening app's search bar or on a podcast website. Subscribing or following it will automatically send new episodes when they become available.

E. Offering a great employee experience

Offering an excellent employee experience is one of the greatest differentiators you can have, impacting everything from workplace culture to productivity levels. Employee satisfaction and engagement play an integral role in your company's profitability. Satisfied employees tend to stay with the business longer, are more productive, and may refer others to your organization.

1. Deliver Excellent Communication

One of the most essential elements for providing an outstanding employee experience is effective communication. Sending messages that align with your company's mission, vision and values will boost morale, boost productivity and reduce workplace miscommunication.

Effective communication tactics require using the appropriate tools, speaking clearly and demonstrating a high level of interest in your audience. Maintaining eye contact and using informal body language are also beneficial strategies.

2. Respond to Feedback

One of the best ways to provide an outstanding employee experience is through feedback. It plays a significant role in any workplace, encouraging accountability, motivating positive change and providing clear objectives and pathways for career growth.

Unfortunately, receiving critical feedback can often lead to intense emotions like anger and defensiveness. To prevent this, take a few moments and carefully process what has been said.

3. Focus on Employees

Employees who feel valued and appreciated at work tend to be more motivated and committed towards reaching the company's objectives. Furthermore, employees will have greater opportunities for engagement with customers, leading to growth in revenue as well as operational excellence.

To provide your employees with an exceptional experience, you should prioritize inspiring leadership, creating an employee-centric culture and streamlining processes using functional technology tailored to your company's requirements. Furthermore, make sure your employee retention rate is high since this will reduce costs associated with recruiting and training new personnel.

4. Promote Diversity and Inclusion

There are many elements that influence employees' satisfaction with their job, but one thing that can make or break a great employee experience is how management treats its team members. Establishing a diverse and inclusive top management team is essential for creating an office culture that values all of its employees' contributions.

To ensure managers understand how to lead a team with individuals of diverse backgrounds, cultures, religions and interests, consider scheduling training on cultural sensitivity.

5. Provide Meaningful Work

A superior employee experience is the cornerstone of retention at your organization. Your workers need to feel connected to their jobs, have faith in management, and have a sense of purpose within the business. Achieving this balance is key for employee success!

People who find meaning in their work tend to experience better health and wellbeing, are more engaged at work, and recover faster from setbacks. That explains why meaningful careers are so commonplace in certain fields - surgeons, clergy members, therapists all find their work to be of immense significance.

6. Make Management Supportive

Managers can foster a sense of safety in the workplace and prevent bullying. Furthermore, managers can offer time off for training courses or events that allow employees to connect with others within the company who share similar interests.

They can also offer support to those going through personal difficulties at home that might affect their work performance. For instance, if an employee is dealing with a family illness, they could be granted time off work to take care of the matter.

7. Create a Positive Work Environment

Establishing a positive work atmosphere encourages employees to come in each day, which in turn results in improved output. It's essential to offer growth opportunities to your employees so they feel like they are developing as individuals. This can be accomplished through various methods, such as mentoring programs or professional development activities.

Regular check-ins with employees, either face to face or virtually, are an effective way to maintain their happiness and engagement at work. Furthermore, it provides them with a chance to share feedback about their experiences.

8. Offer Growth Opportunities

Growth opportunities at work are one of the best ways to keep your employees satisfied and engaged. They don't have to be expensive; they could simply involve providing training or allowing staff members to take a course on their own time.

Growth is about being challenged and stretched. It also involves developing new skills that you can apply in both professional and personal life.

X. Continuously Improving and Learning

A. Encouraging innovation

Innovation is an essential aspect of business, helping a company stand out from others and increase revenue and market share. To promote innovation, organizations should make it a core value. Doing this will motivate employees to be more creative and daring in their work.

Make Innovation a Core Value

Innovation is a critical element of business success. It helps companies stay ahead of the competition in an ever-evolving market, creates value and increases brand recognition.

The top companies strive to innovate in order to satisfy their customers' needs. They do this by recognizing customer issues and finding solutions. Innovation can be used to develop new products and services, enhance existing ones or reduce costs. Businesses may use innovation to boost revenue and capture more market share.

Hire People with Different Perspectives

Diversity of talent is a great asset for any company, as it fosters creativity and strategic thinking when employees from different backgrounds come together to tackle problems.

Harvard Business Review research has demonstrated that diversity in the workplace leads to higher innovation rates. Indeed, inclusive companies are 1.7 times more likely to be thought leaders within their industry! However, sometimes a cohesive team can become stagnant. That is why it's beneficial to bring in new blood who will challenge the status quo and provide fresh perspectives.

Give Your Employees Time and Space

If you want your employees to be able to think creatively and innovate at work, then you must give them the space and time to do so. Without this, they won't be able to come up with solutions that make your business more efficient and profitable. Many forward-thinking companies provide employees with time to create new ideas. This could be done through an employee retreat, regular allocating of time in their day or a dedicated innovation vacation.

Encourage Collaboration

Collaboration is the key to driving innovation, as everyone brings their own special skills and ideas to the table. By welcoming these differences, you can generate new concepts that can propel your business forward.

Collaboration requires effective execution if it's going to succeed. Establishing ground rules and objectives beforehand will help keep the process organized. Furthermore, it's essential to promote teamwork and reward employees for their contributions. Doing so not only motivates people to collaborate but also demonstrates that their ideas are valued.

Have a Feedback Process

One of the best ways to foster innovation in your business is through having a feedback process. This can help your team members comprehend how they are performing on their job and what needs improvement. Additionally, it can assist them in progressing within their careers.

Positive reinforcement can motivate employees to work harder and faster.

Feedback should be specific, constructive and objective. It should also be tied to a particular goal or behavior so the receiver understands why they are receiving that particular feedback and what action steps can be taken regarding it.

Implement Ideas as Soon as Possible

One of the best ways to foster innovation is ensuring ideas are implemented promptly. This approach is especially relevant for frontline employees who may have a unique insight on how to address problems that directly impact them.

Implementing the ideas of your employees quickly not only boosts employee morale and productivity, but it also promotes employee satisfaction and cohesion - leading to reduced turnover as well.

Reward Employees for Their Ideas

Rewarding employees for their innovative ideas is a necessary component of creating an innovation culture. However, make sure the rewards offered align with your organization's values.

For instance, hosting a pizza party or happy hour might be fun for one employee but embarrass those who prefer quiet work environments. On the other hand, rewarding someone with a coveted parking spot might reward those who seek prestige but might embarrass those who do not enjoy being on display.

B. Developing a strong online presence

Establishing a robust online presence is essential for any business, whether you're an established brand or just starting out. It helps potential customers locate you, engage with you and build trust in your brand. It can be a time-consuming endeavor, so having an effective strategy in place is key. But don't fret - there are plenty of approaches you can use for success.

Build an Email List

If you want to build a powerful online presence, having an email list is essential. This is an effective and affordable way to spread your marketing messages to current customers and prospective clients.

To expand your email list, you can utilize various tactics like homepage pop-up forms, sales and discounts. However, if you want to build it quickly and efficiently, it's essential that you do it correctly.

Master SEO

Establishing a robust online presence is essential for growing your business and reaching new clients. It allows for easy discovery when potential clients search for products and services you provide. A successful SEO strategy will assist in reaching this objective. It involves employing best practices that will boost your website's organic search engine ranking.

Maintaining an effective SEO strategy can be daunting, but it's essential to stay abreast of industry changes and the most up-to-date tactics. Keep an eye out for Google Webmaster Central Blog posts and other expert resources like HubSpot's SEO newsletter for assistance.

Create Value

Establishing a robust online presence is essential for any business. Maintaining an up-to-date and relevant website can help you foster trust with your followers. Value creation involves offering customers useful products and services that they consider worth their time, energy and money. It also involves maximizing benefits at an acceptable price point.

Be Active Online

Establishing a robust online presence is essential for any small business' marketing plan. Not only does it help you stand out from your competition, but it can also boost your visibility to potential customers.

Though it may be challenging to carve out enough time for consistent and successful online presence, there are a few key strategies you can employ. With these tactics in place, you should see an impressive improvement in your online presence over time.

Analyze Your Results

Building a robust online presence can be intimidating, especially in today's highly competitive market. But it is an essential aspect for making sure your business stays connected to customers and prospects. Analyzing your results is the best way to determine how successful your efforts are. This will enable you to identify which strategies work, which don't, and where improvements can be made in future. Furthermore, it ensures that you make use of all available time and resources efficiently.

Adopt New Forums

Online forums are an invaluable tool for cultivating customer relationships. Not only do they reduce your customer support team's workload, but they provide visitors with a safe space to voice their issues in confidence.

Establishing a successful forum necessitates careful preparation and execution. Here are some tips to keep in mind:

Have a Social Media Presence

Establishing a robust online presence is essential for any business. With the rise in usage of social media platforms, those without an account on these networks are missing out on an expansive audience of potential customers.

When done correctly, your social media presence can help build brand awareness, engage with your community and expose your products to a wide array of new buyers. It also serves as an effective way for you to establish personal connections with your target audience, letting them know who you are and what values you hold dear.

Make a Website

Establishing a powerful online presence is essential for cultivating your brand image and increasing brand recognition. Furthermore, it fosters trust between potential customers. To make your website stand out from the competition, select a design that is attractive and user-friendly. Furthermore, ensure it contains relevant keywords and content to boost search engine rankings. Your website's pages should reflect the different facets of your business, such as Home, About Us, Contact, Privacy Policy and Terms and Conditions.

C. Fostering transparency and open communication

Fostering transparency and open communication in your organization can improve employee morale, boost productivity, and build trust. However, this process can also prove challenging; leaders need to strike a balance between transparency and privacy.

Establishing channels of communication between managers and their direct reports to encourage feedback is essential. Furthermore, leaders must be transparent when conveying major decisions or challenges to their team members.

Make the information digestible

When communicating information to your audience, it should be easy for them to absorb. Furthermore, make sure the language used is suitable; this will guarantee better comprehension rates.

Make your longform content more digestible by breaking it up into sections with headings. Doing this will give readers a quick summary of the key points and encourage them to read more of your material. Another tool that will aid your readers' comprehension is visuals. This could be in the form of an eye-catching infographic or even just an image with a brief quote.

Create information that's easily digestible, so your audience reads and shares it. Doing this not only leads to better marketing results but also improves the quality of your data. So be sure to take this into consideration when crafting your next piece of content!

Actively listen

If you want to promote transparency and open communication, practicing active listening is essential. This communication skill can be applied in many contexts and forms part of emotional intelligence. Active listening teaches you to listen with empathy and without judgment, helping you build a positive rapport with others and increasing trust between team members.

Delegating responsibility effectively can also help you manage conflict effectively. When your team members feel like you are truly listening to their needs and worries, they are more likely to join in finding solutions together. Active listening can be enhanced through practice and feedback, but you should start by practicing in everyday situations like conversations with coworkers or when interviewing for a new job. When participating in these conversations, pay close attention to what the other person says and demonstrate your engagement by nodding your head, maintaining eye contact, or giving small verbal responses such as "yes" or "huh". These small gestures show you're paying attention and showing that you are engaged in the conversation.

Meet people where they are

One of the most effective ways to promote transparency and open communication is by meeting people where they are. While this may sound straightforward, working with people from various backgrounds or fields can present unique challenges.

First and foremost, you need to comprehend their personal struggles. This requires meeting them where they are emotionally, mentally and physically. Second, you need to help them identify what's preventing them from reaching their own goals and strengths. This can often be done through assessment rather than judgment.

Particularly when working with community members, understanding their individual challenges and potential solutions is paramount. No matter if it's an individual needing to talk about their issues or an organization striving to increase its social impact, you must comprehend their situation and how best you can assist them in realizing it.

Be open to hard truths

No matter the situation, transparency and open communication are paramount for forming lasting and rewarding relationships. A lack of openness can lead to confusion, misunderstandings, and even conflict; so making sure you get the right information to the right people at the right time is paramount for your success.

Transparent communication is key, and for successful results. A balanced approach should be taken when selecting between live and virtual options for communicating with colleagues. Ultimately, selecting the most suitable online communication platform depends on your work requirements as well as how you prefer to be reached.

For example, if your profession necessitates constant communication with clients, chat rooms might be your ideal option. On the other hand, video conferencing or virtual meetings offer more privacy and offer everyone something they can benefit from - especially when working in a high performance team with excellent communication abilities.

D. Utilizing customer data and insights

Insights about your consumers are the conclusions you get from analyzing the information you gather about them across all of your channels of communication. Customer comments and form submissions are examples of direct data collection, whereas website analytics and loyalty programme participation are examples of inferred data collection.

There are a plethora of quantitative and qualitative measures that may be used to analyze consumer insights, and the ones that are most relevant to your company and target audience will vary. Only 16% of teams, according to GetApp's study, have enough data but lack the necessary insights.

The value of understanding your target audience in marketing

Buyer personas are fictional characters that represent your ideal customers. To create them, you need information about your customers, such as their demographics, their pain points, what they find impressive and what they find disappointing, how often they buy products or services, what factors influence their purchasing decisions, and so on.

Your ability to Analyze data will improve with the amount of research you put into your target market.

- Do not miss an opportunity to send a timely message.
- Exhibit the appropriate goods at the appropriate cost.
- Emphasize the elements that will most appeal to your target audience.
- Practice compassion and connecting with others on an emotional level.
- Improve your one and only selling point.
- Use data to refine your strategies and tailor your messages.

In turn, this will maintain high levels of customer happiness, decrease churn, enhance loyalty, and more as part of a successful growth marketing plan.

Insights from customers: where and how to get them

While gathering consumer insights may seem like looking for a needle in a haystack, the signal can be isolated from the noise if one knows where and how to look. Listed below are 10 such resources, along with some pointers on making the most of them.

1. Feedback on the Web

One of the most reliable ways to gauge consumer satisfaction is via reviews posted on third-party websites. Use them to learn what consumers like about your brand, what they wish you would change, and what they like better from competitors.

Included in this category are testimonials posted about you online. G2, Capterra, Clutch, Trustpilot, and TrustRadius are among the most well-known software/SaaS rating websites. These require the reviewer to sign up using their existing social media account, giving us confidence that the reviews are from real people.

What to do with the information you find in customer reviews:

Discover which details are most memorable to your consumers and use them to improve your service. Monitor customer feedback to learn where your product or service may be falling short.

Take the time to learn the language your target audience uses to express their issues and wants so you can address them directly in your marketing materials.

2. Feedback on rivals

Just as how you can learn about your target market from the feedback left on rivals' websites, you can do the same thing with review websites. These may exist on the aforementioned websites or in social media groups dedicated to the product in question.

According to The Blog Starter's creator and B2B consultant Scott Chow:

"You may go deeper into customer evaluations to get a feel on what expectations consumers had when signing up for competing products and what they really received."

Search for voids that your service can fill. Use what you've learned to inform your product's positioning and marketing. More leads will result from this since your products and services will more closely match those of your target audience.

Methods for drawing useful information from critiques of competitors:

- ❖ See where they fall short, then fill the void.
- ❖ Examine their advantages over your own and figure out how to counter them using our SWOT analysis template.
- ❖ Collect inspiration for user-appreciated functions and actions.
3. **Information from a Website**

Using Google's free tools like Analytics and Search Console, you may learn a great deal about your clientele, such as:

- Information about your visitors' actions, such as the search terms they used to find your site, the pathways they take while navigating it, the pages they leave on, the kind of material that piques their interest, and so on.

- Indicators of a person's identity, such as age, gender, location, hobbies, and technology use.
- Information gathered from a campaign, including the pages that generate the most interest and sales, conversion rates, and other useful metrics.

Therefore, it is crucial to create a website and have all of your marketing efforts direct people there.

Gaining valuable insights from website visitor data:

- Figure out the search terms and subject areas you want to cover.
- See which sites they're leaving to see whether an exit popup or other call to action is necessary.
- Research several variations of your landing page's text to find out which ones result in the most click-throughs.
- Determine which methods are more fruitful and invest more heavily there.

- Affinity categories in Google Analytics: A Tool for Collecting Customer Insights. One of the many useful pieces of information you can get from Google Analytics is the visitors' Affinity Categories.

4. **Information from rival websites**

Competitor websites won't provide as much data, but SEO tools like Semrush and Ahrefs will provide you a wealth of information. If you own a design firm and Venngage is one of your competitors, you can use Ahrefs to see what keywords they're using in their content and advertisements. Techniques for Gathering Information from Customers Through Keyword Research on Competitors

Based on the data above, it's evident that Venngage users like having access to premade content. You might expand your services to include this or shift your market position to accommodate it.

5. **Shopping habits and individual tastes**

The buying habits of your consumers provide you with invaluable insight about the items and services that are most in demand. If you have a customer relationship management system or an online storefront, you will have access to this data. In addition, preference centers may be made for email lists and other account-required platforms in order to get even more direct information.

A little aside: as you can see, this piece is going to include a lot of data. Accordingly, make sure you are well-versed on the finest methods for keeping your clients' information safe.

6. Surveys of Customers

Although companies have utilized surveys since the days of door-to-door marketing, the advent of internet survey technologies has made it much easier to distribute surveys through email, social media, apps, and other channels. In terms of survey formats, you're free to mix and match point scales, multiple choice questions, and free-form comments. To get the most out of your survey campaign, it's important to divide respondents into subgroups based on characteristics like whether they are new customers, long-time customers, top referrers, or disengaged.

Consider the following as potential survey questions:

- Tell me how you heard about us.
- To what extent did you like it?
- Ordering Simplicity
- Providing Assistance to Clients
- Pricing v/sPackaging
- Additional Factors
- Please tell us where we can do better.

In addition, you may use the NPS survey, which consists of just one question.

"How likely are you to suggest our company to a friend or colleague on a scale of 0 to 10?"

7. Consultations with Clients

An interview with a consumer is more personalized than a poll delivered to a large group of customers. There are a few different ways to conduct them: in person, over the phone, or through video chat. With these, you may elicit detailed responses from clients who otherwise would not take the time to send you a lengthy survey response.

Things that can be spoken about are:

- Tell me how you heard about us.
- Why did you choose us instead of other options?
- To what extent does your company make use of it ?
- Please tell us what we can do to improve our product.

"Customer conversations enable you to explore deeper on the go and acquire deeper insights, something you can't do with surveys," says Assaf Cohen, CEO of game company Solitaire Bliss. By conducting consumer interviews, we learned that multiplayer games are particularly popular because of their social aspects.

8. Examples of what works and case studies

Customer interviews might also take the shape of anecdotes about past successes, recommendations, or case studies. This one, though, is not about what your customers think; rather, it's about the issue you helped them address with your products or services. Materials aimed at the general population may be either textual or aural/visual.

In general, a success narrative will try to address the following questions:

- What issue were you trying to solve? Exactly what were the repercussions?
- To begin with, we're curious as to how you came across us and what drew you to work with us specifically.
- Tell me about the service or product you used to have the issue fixed.
- How did it work out, and what good did it do?
- Examples of Marketing Case Studies the lintel

Applying lessons learned from satisfied customers:

- Offer at first consultations and presentations.
- Incorporate them on your website for others to look over.
- Develop and pitch targeted use cases to target audiences.

9. Cooperatives

In today's interconnected digital economy, few goods and services can stand on their own. In technical terms, this means making nice with other services and programmes.

Software as a service (SaaS) payment solutions, for instance, may seek integration with other types of business applications, such as invoicing, proposal, accounting, and sales tools. As a group, you may work to boost the product's overall appeal while also learning from one another's experiences.

Partnerships as a means of gaining knowledge about your customers and how to utilize that information

- Develop novel contests and freebies to offer.

- Try looking for related subjects to write about.
- Discover potential enhancements and extras.
- Ten. Online networking

Social media is an excellent area to get insights from customers since people are not shy about sharing their experiences, whether they be positive or negative. You may keep an ear out for feedback by reading comments and postings, and you can actively seek it out by posting polls and other types of open-ended questions (you can learn how to gather intel using Instagram Story polls here).

Your social media metrics are a gold mine of information about your audience. Keep in mind that the people who follow you on social media could be somewhat different from the people who become your customers.

Advice on gleaning useful information from social media about your target audience:

- Learn to think like your consumers and speak their language.

- Try to put yourself in their shoes and try to feel what they're feeling.
- Discover what people are looking for and what they like.

Consider the feedback of your customers and use it.

With customer insights, you can filter out the irrelevant channels, positioning, services, and message and zero in on the ones that will have the most impact on your business. However, they are not a unified file accessible from a single source. To achieve this, you need to assemble them from various channels; fortunately, modern digital marketing provides the means to do so.

E. Offering exceptional after-sales support

After-sales support is an innovative marketing tactic businesses use to foster customer loyalty, boost sales, and attract new clients. The type of after-sales support available depends on the product. It could be provided by the manufacturer, retailer, or even a third party.

Show your appreciation

Offering excellent after-sales support can boost customer confidence and security about their purchase, leading them to stay with your business longer and increasing their lifetime value. According to Vande Walle, customer appreciation should be a top priority across your entire organization in order to be successful. Customers' feelings of gratitude and appreciation are directly connected to their satisfaction levels and loyalty levels - so making customer appreciation an organizational priority is critical for long-term success.

Instead of simply sending customers an email or giving them a gift, take the time to understand what your customers are likely most passionate about from your brand and then craft a customer appreciation strategy that aligns with their preferences.

Provide pre-installation services

One of the best ways to increase customer retention rates is by providing excellent after-sales support. This could range from an automated chatbot to a free demo of a new software product. Furthermore, taking time out to get to know your customers better allows for personalized communication tailored to their individual needs.

It's no secret that customers are more likely to make purchases if they feel confident in your ability to provide them with an effortless buying experience. Delivering an outstanding after-sales experience not only retains current customers, but it can also win you the trust and loyalty of potential new ones as well. The most effective way to accomplish this is by focusing on who your ideal customer is and then giving them what they need. Furthermore, make sure your team has all of the skill sets and resources necessary for delivering a superior customer experience.

Have excellent customer service

After-sales support can increase customer retention and motivate people to purchase from you again. It also contributes to building a strong brand image that will keep customers pleased, leading them to recommend your products to their friends and family.

Your customer service team should be able to answer questions quickly and clearly across multiple channels, such as phone, email, messaging, live chat, social media platforms and more. Furthermore, they must understand their customers' preferred methods for contact so that they can provide the most helpful response possible. Acquiring essential customer service skills does not come naturally. It takes years of practice and learning from errors. Therefore, investing time and resources into your team's training for customer service is essential; furthering these lessons through ongoing reinforcement through ongoing instruction and support.

Give your customers initial user training

One of the best ways to ensure your customers are familiar with your product is by providing initial user training. This could include product tutorials and guided walkthroughs.

Utilizing these tools can assist your customers in getting the most out of your product, making it simpler for them to reach their objectives. This may lead to increased revenue and a higher customer retention rate.

The initial step in developing your training program is to identify the training needs of your customers. This can be done through a series of user interviews or surveys.

F Continuously educating yourself

Maintaining one's knowledge base is an essential habit for anyone to pursue. It also serves to keep you ahead of the competition in the job market. It requires a keen interest, the capacity for focus and an eagerness to learn. Furthermore, discipline and motivation are necessary.

Stay Current on Industry News

Staying abreast of industry news can make you a stronger leader and maximize the opportunities that present themselves in your career. One of the best ways to stay current with industry trends is through reading professional journals and blogs. These free online resources often contain scholarly research and content relevant to your field of work.

Social media is another useful source for industry news. By following experts and industry leaders on Twitter, Instagram or LinkedIn, you'll stay up to date with the most up-to-date data.

Sign Up for Online Courses

Online courses can be an excellent way to develop and polish your skills and knowledge. They offer the convenience of learning at your own pace and may be more cost-effective than attending campus classes. Making the most of your online learning experience requires selecting a course that matches both your preferences and personality. This includes selecting either synchronous or asynchronous instruction; understanding the costs associated with taking an online course; and selecting an appropriate course provider.

A good online course should fulfill its promises and have high-quality content tailored to you and your career objectives. This makes the experience more enjoyable and provides valuable insights into what you are studying.

Get a Mentor

Mentorship is one of the most essential ways to stay educated. They'll open your mind to new possibilities, challenge your preconceptions and impart invaluable life lessons. They will also equip you with the abilities and mindset necessary for success in your professional career. A great mentor should possess a wide range of expertise and be eager to share it with you. They shouldn't be someone who reluctantly gives away knowledge without expecting payment in return, nor should they reveal things in an unclear or manipulative manner.

Your mentor should have a discussion with you about their goals and what can be expected from the relationship. Additionally, make sure to follow up regularly to receive feedback on how things are progressing in your relationship.

Take Up an Arts Class

Enrolling in an arts class is a great way to stay educated. Not only does it develop your creative abilities, but it has been known to reduce stress levels throughout the body as well. No matter your skill level or artistic experience, taking an art class can be a great way to expand your knowledge and master new techniques. Plus, with so many online courses available, finding the ideal one for you won't be hard!

The initial step in learning something new is to identify what it is that interests you. Doing this will help narrow down your search and eliminate classes that don't provide a focus on what it is you wish to gain knowledge about.

Start Journaling

Journaling can be an excellent tool for continuing education. It promotes learning and reflection, making it a fun habit that you'll want to keep up with. Begin by setting aside some time each day to write in your journal. It could be morning, afternoon or night - whatever works best for you! If you're having difficulty staying motivated, try using a timer. This could be as easy as wearing your watch or smartphone and will help ensure that you stay on track.

You could also create a weekly journal review, where you read through entries and reflect on what has been learned. Doing this will help you retain and apply your insights.

XI. Inspiring and Empowering Your Team

A. Encouraging open communication

Open communication is an effective way to empower your employees and get them speaking up. It can help you avoid major issues and foster stronger bonds with your team members. Open communication is essential for maintaining healthy relationships and producing quality work, but it can also present challenges. Leaders sometimes unintentionally do things that actually hinder open communication from taking place.

Be transparent from the top down.

Leaders who are open and honest create an atmosphere of trust among employees, leading to higher levels of performance. Transparency is also a powerful way to build relationships within teams. Establishing strong bonds between leadership and employees promotes collaboration and problem-solving abilities.

Employees feel more fulfilled when they know they are employed by a company with high ethical standards and open communication, as this will give them the sense that their efforts contribute to something bigger than themselves alone. Promoting transparency within your company is the most efficient way to promote it. This involves encouraging daily standups and communicating information across departments.

Ask employees for feedback.

Receiving feedback from employees is an integral part of creating a healthy workplace culture. It provides valuable insight into how your team functions and can help improve areas of the business that require improvement.

Many companies employ formal processes for collecting employee feedback, but managers should feel empowered to solicit ongoing, real-time input from their teams. When seeking feedback, be deliberate with the questions you pose. General and vague queries rarely yield insightful responses from your team members.

Show respect for your employees when they provide honest, candid feedback. Dan Hassell, founder of Feedback Coaching, suggests that when employees provide honest feedback, don't hesitate to acknowledge it and respond politely.

Demonstrate respect for employees.

Employees who feel they can trust a leader are more likely to share their ideas and suggestions. Therefore, it is essential for leaders to model appropriate behavior so that employees feel confident doing so as well.

Be approachable and demonstrate that you care about each employee on a personal level, regardless of their role within the organization. Small gestures like sending them a cheerful morning greeting or remembering their birthdays can help foster an encouraging atmosphere within your workplace.

Demonstrating respect is a proven way to encourage open communication. Employees are more likely to feel free to voice their opinions when managers acknowledge them, even if it may not always be possible to act upon them immediately.

Tackle problems head-on.

Companies with a well-rounded team can gain many advantages by cultivating an open communication culture. It is the single most essential factor in maintaining an engaged and productive workforce. While getting everyone on the same page may prove challenging at first, making this priority will result in healthier financial results as well as contented employees.

Promoting open communication on your team is the best way to promote it. Encourage them to speak up and ask what they need in order to be successful, or you could enlist the assistance of an experienced employee coach who can guide you through teamwork's complex terrain. A good coach can be invaluable, particularly during times of stress or crisis.

Get to know others on a personal level.

If you want to promote open communication, an effective first step is getting to know people on a personal level. That way, you can better comprehend how to build and sustain healthy relationships. Some of us may be born socially comfortable, yet others may struggle to connect on a deeper level. Studies show that many people prefer small talk and avoid meaningful conversations due to fears of them being awkward or insensitive.

That is why it is essential to be approachable socially and show others you are interested in them. Do this by maintaining eye contact, keeping your head up, and not blocking other people with objects like drinks or phones.

B. Offering opportunities for growth and development

Offering your team opportunities for growth and development can be a powerful factor in increasing productivity and morale. This could take the form of continuous professional development or creating tailored individual development plans.

CPD, or continuing professional development, allows professionals to maintain the skills and knowledge necessary for success in their profession. It may also serve as a means of staying abreast of current developments and trends within their sector.

Offer continuous professional development

Offering your team opportunities for growth and development is a great way to keep them engaged. It demonstrates that your organization values their career advancement and is invested in keeping them with you long-term.

Continuing professional development (CPD) is the process of maintaining and improving one's skills, knowledge and experience by actively tracking learning activities that lead to improved performance. This can be accomplished through formal courses, webinars, conferences, coaching/mentoring services, external certifications or degrees as well as informal learning opportunities.

CPD also encourages employees to reflect on their progress, which can be an invaluable asset for growth and development. Whether it's by writing in a journal or taking time to analyze data in Excel, taking the time to reflect can help you gain greater insight into your practice and identify areas for improvement. Continuous professional development (CPD) is beneficial for both you and your employees, but can be challenging to implement on a large scale. To guarantee its success, carefully plan and execute the CPD program accordingly.

Create individualized development plans

Individualized development plans are an invaluable tool to help employees set short and long-term objectives, as well as identify the training and other developmental opportunities necessary to reach them. These documents represent a collaborative effort between employees and their manager to enhance professional skill sets.

Supervisors, take the time to develop and implement an individualized development plan for each member of your team. Doing so will ensure all employees are on the same page when it comes to their career objectives, which in turn, can serve as motivation for them to stay with the company.

An Individual Development Plan (IDP) should be reviewed periodically for maximum benefit. As you progress in your career and gain expertise, consider adding new objectives and strategies to your plan.

Help your team improve soft skills

To keep your team productive, engaged and committed, providing opportunities for growth and development should be at the top of your priority list. One way to do this is by encouraging employees to take on challenges outside their usual duties and responsibilities.

When employees feel challenged by their tasks, it can help them develop essential soft skills like teamwork, time management and leadership potential. Acquiring these skills is essential in today's diverse workplace, where employees must be able to collaborate with people of varying backgrounds and cultures.

You can help your employees develop and enhance these essential abilities through various training programs. Team-building exercises can improve communication and collaboration, while conflict resolution instruction teaches workers how to efficiently resolve workplace disputes.

Remove barriers

Offering opportunities for growth and development to your team can have a beneficial effect on their performance and engagement at work. But it's essential that you remove any obstacles that prevent employees from taking advantage of these chances you provide them.

Establishing specific professional development goals for your team and setting clear expectations to reach those objectives is essential to guarantee they don't feel overwhelmed with tasks, while helping them focus on their desired result. Employees who take a growth-oriented approach are more likely to recognize the rewards of development and strive hard for them. They understand that success doesn't always come easily, so they don't hesitate to try again until they succeed.

Identification and removal of obstacles that prevent your team from taking advantage of professional development opportunities can have a powerful impact on their performance, engagement and motivation. By eliminating these roadblocks, you give them the tools they need to reach their objectives while increasing productivity and business profitability.

C. Recognizing and rewarding hard work

Recognizing and rewarding hard work is an effective way to motivate employees, enhance productivity, boost morale, and foster strong workplace relationships. Thankfully, there are numerous ways to promote employee wellness in your company. The key is finding something that works for both your team and company culture.

Make Travel More Comfortable

Long flights can be daunting, but there are ways to make them less tedious. This is especially true if your team is highly motivated. From hosting a round-the-clock booze cruise to giving employees an impressive swag bag filled with treats, there are many low-key yet high impact ways to show your employees how much you value them.

With the right employees, you can craft an unforgettable experience that will remain in their memories for years to come. Most importantly, make it fun and exciting!

Gift Cards

Gift cards are an ideal way to recognize and reward your employees for their hard work.

Not only are they budget friendly, but they make recipients feel truly appreciated which in turn promotes employee engagement and retention.

Many businesses provide cash-based rewards, but they often lack the personal and memorable elements that gift cards provide. This may lead recipients to perceive them as salary increases rather than acknowledgement of their accomplishments.

Company Merchandise

Recognizing and rewarding hard work is an effective way to demonstrate your appreciation for employees. Doing so will encourage them to keep striving towards your company's objectives, giving them motivation and boosting morale within the workplace.

One of the best ways to promote your business is through company merchandise. This promotional item bears your business' name or logo and is often given away free of charge. By providing employees with branded items, you can help them build emotional connections to the company and recall its core objectives and values. These mementos will serve as reminders of what the business stands for and help reinforce what it stands for.

Community Building Activities

When employees do a great job, it is essential to recognize and reward them. There are numerous ways of accomplishing this. One way to recognize and reward hard work of your employees is by sharing their accomplishments on social media platforms like Twitter, LinkedIn or the company's webpages. Show your appreciation for their success today!

Create a sense of community in your classroom by participating in activities with children that promote socialization, problem-solving and new experiences. These engaging exercises will bring out the best in students.

WFH/Flexi-timing

Employees work tirelessly to make their organization successful, so it is essential to acknowledge and reward them for all that they do. Offering WFH/Flexi-timing is one great way to do this.

Flexible scheduling provides employees with the freedom to balance their lives, which is something everyone appreciates in today's hectic world. Furthermore, it gives them more time for family obligations and other significant events in their lives.

Celebrate Career Landmarks

Recognizing and rewarding employees for their hard work is one of the best ways to boost employee retention. Not only that, but it can also lift morale in your workplace. Employees who have achieved a career milestone or done something special in their work life can be immensely proud and happy with their accomplishments. Celebrating these moments serves to recognize their hard work and give them an opportunity to feel appreciated for their efforts.

Some companies have created employee recognition pages, where employees' successes are showcased for all to see. This is an effective way of showing your employees that you value their success and serving as a permanent reminder of how they've contributed to the company.

Office Space

Rewarding employees for their hard work can be an effective way to motivate them. Offering them a comfortable workspace is another great reward for those who have done their jobs well. A small office space can offer employees privacy when working on sensitive projects. Furthermore, it helps reduce distractions which in turn increases productivity levels.

If you want to make your workspace more employee-friendly, it is essential that you consult them first about their preferences before making any modifications. Doing this will maximize productivity within your team while keeping them content.

D. Providing support and resources for mental and physical well-being

Mental health is more than simply not having a mental illness. It's about managing your emotions and behavior in a healthy manner so that you can live a full and rewarding life.

Connecting to people and the world is also about feeling valued and having a sense of belonging. Maintaining strong, supportive relationships will give you that feeling of value and belonging that so many strive for.

Get Regular Exercise

Exercising is an invaluable medicine that helps combat health issues, increases energy levels, builds strength and relieves stress. Not only that but it helps you maintain a healthy body weight as well as regulates your appetite.

Exercising regularly can benefit both mental and physical wellbeing. To begin, start slowly and increase the time spent exercising as soon as you feel comfortable. Your doctor can assist in crafting an individualized program tailored towards you that works for you.

Eat Healthy

Eating nutritious, regular meals and staying hydrated are essential for your mental and physical wellbeing. These habits can improve your mood as well as provide you with energy throughout the day.

Eating a balanced diet that includes fruits, vegetables, whole grains and low-fat protein can help lower the risk of chronic diseases like heart disease, cancer and diabetes. Consulting with a registered dietitian for advice on making healthier food choices may also be beneficial.

Stay Hydrated

Maintaining adequate fluid intake is one of the most essential steps you can take for improved overall wellbeing. Hydration helps your body's normal processes, such as temperature regulation and blood pressure regulation, plus detoxification processes. To maintain electrolytes balance, aim to drink 48 to 64 ounces of fluids daily - approximately six or eight glasses.

Make Sleep a Priority

Sleeping enough is critical for both mental and physical wellbeing. It can improve moods, increase concentration levels and help manage feelings of anxiety or depression.

Sleep is so essential, yet it can be challenging to prioritize it in your busy schedule. But you don't have to miss out on quality snooze time each day - make time for it today!

Try a Relaxing Activity

Relaxing can be a great way to reduce stress and anxiety. It doesn't need to take up much time, but even just a few minutes of relaxation can help you feel more at peace.

Progressive muscle relaxation (PMR) is a simple method for relieving muscular tension. Combining it with other techniques can help you reach an enhanced state of mental relaxation.

Set Goals and Priorities

One way to prioritize your mental and physical well-being is setting goals. Goals are essential as they keep you focused on the right things while preventing distractions from outside sources.

Setting goals is the first step to achieving them. However, this can be challenging when there are many competing demands on your time or things that conflict with each other.

Practice Gratitude

Gratitude is an easy yet powerful way to enhance your mental and physical wellbeing. Research has demonstrated that practicing gratitude can reduce stress, lower blood pressure, and enhance sleep quality.

One of the most effective ways to express gratitude is writing a letter or email to someone you are thankful for, whether that be someone at work, a friend, or family member. Writing such a letter or email can be especially effective when there are multiple people involved.

Focus on Positivity

A positive outlook in life can make a profound impact on both mental and physical wellbeing. It may reduce the risk of heart disease, boost immunity, improve sleep quality, and even assist with fighting depression.

However, it's essential to find the balance between positive thinking and negative thoughts. Excessively positive thinking (known as toxic positivity) can have an adverse effect on your mental wellbeing.

Stay Connected

Maintaining healthy connections is one of the most essential elements for mental and physical well being. Establishing strong connections with friends, family and coworkers can reduce anxiety and depression symptoms, boost self-esteem levels and enhance quality of life overall. Phone and video calls are an ideal way to stay in touch with loved ones, particularly if they live far away. Physical contact such as hugging someone can have a beneficial effect on human connection and health as well.

XII. Financial Management

A. Creating a budget and financial projections

Establishing a budget and making financial projections are essential steps for anyone wishing to effectively manage their finances. This is especially relevant when attempting to meet short and long term objectives such as saving money for a down payment on a car or home, investing in retirement accounts or paying off debt.

Calculate Your Net Income

An effective budget begins with net income, which is the amount left over after subtracting taxes and other deductions. This includes everything from your salary to interest on savings accounts or any other sources of income you receive outside of traditional paychecks.

The 50-20-30 Rule suggests that 50% of your net income should go toward living expenses and essentials (Needs), 20% should go toward debt reduction and savings, and 30% for discretionary spending (Wants). This ratio helps you create a predictable budget by guaranteeing you can pay all bills each month without having to dip into the Wants category.

Business accounting software can assist in tracking net income and other financial metrics for your company, making it simpler to spot trends or potential issues in the company's finances.

Track Your Spending

Establishing a budget and financial projections are essential, but they only work if you keep track of your spending. Tracking your spending is a great way to do so. Reviewing bank and credit card statements from the previous month can help you identify expenses that might be leading you to spend too much, as well as identify strategies for cost-cutting.

Tracking your spending with various apps is now easier than ever. They connect to both bank and investment accounts, allowing you to see how each expense fits into the overall budget.

Set Realistic Goals

Budgeting and making financial projections are great tools to get your spending under control, but to make them truly effective you need to set achievable objectives.

Begin by considering what you want out of life and how you would like to allocate your finances. Create a goal that is specific, measurable, achievable, realistic with an agreed upon timeline. Now, write down your goals on a worksheet and label each one as either "critical," "need," or "want" so that you know which funds to fund next.

Short-term goals are those you must reach within one year, such as creating an emergency fund or paying off credit card debt. Longer-term objectives take years or even decades to accomplish, such as saving for retirement or your child's education.

Make a Plan

Budgeting and making financial projections are essential elements of personal finance management. They allow you to prioritize spending, save money for important goals, and manage debt more effectively. An effective budget begins with net income, which is the difference between your total income and total expenses. This number serves as the starting point for all other budgeting tasks and financial projections.

Track your spending by getting a receipt for every expense you make during a month - such as food, restaurants and entertainment. You can also utilize your bank's online-banking features to monitor spending in more detail.

Once you have an accurate understanding of your spending, it's time to set achievable objectives. These can range from saving for a vacation, paying off debts or creating an emergency fund.

Adjust Your Spending

An effective budget starts with your net income, which is the amount taken home from work after any deductions have been taken. This figure serves as a key indicator of a company's financial health and is frequently used by investors and creditors when determining whether it can pay dividends or settle debt obligations.

The next step in creating a budget is to keep track of your spending. Begin by separating fixed expenses (like rent or mortgage) from variable costs. If your fixed expenses exceed your net income, it could be time to reduce some of those costs. For instance, switching phone providers or shopping around for a cheaper energy bill can save money each month.

It's wise to review your budget periodically. A major life event such as a new job or the arrival of a child can drastically alter your lifestyle and necessitate changes in the budget.

B. Monitoring cash flow and financial performance

Monitoring cash flow and financial performance are essential elements for running a successful business. It helps you stay abreast of your needs and guarantee that there's enough money to fund growth initiatives. Maintaining accurate inventory records is essential for cash flow management. It helps you decide when to order more inventory or replace it.

Essential financial statements

Financial statements give a snapshot of your business' health and are essential for tracking cash flow and performance. When managers from multiple departments review these documents, they gain a better insight into their company's condition, which in turn can guide goal setting and budgeting processes.

The balance sheet is the most critical of these statements, displaying three essential items: assets, liabilities and equity. This representation allows users to assess a company's current worth and is also utilized by financial analysts when calculating essential ratios.

Aged Debtors' Trial Balance

An Aged Debtors' Trial Balance is a report that displays all of a business's outstanding receivables over time. It helps monitor cash flow and financial performance, as well as allow companies to estimate how many bad debts may become due in the future.

These reports are typically generated at the end of each month to provide an overview of invoices that remain unpaid. Companies use these reports to prioritize collections efforts and guarantee they're following up with customers promptly.

Inventory records

Inventory records enable businesses to monitor stock levels, purchase new merchandise and ensure an adequate supply of products. They also enable companies to identify fast-moving and slow-moving items so they can anticipate sales trends and prepare for surges in demand. Maintaining an organized inventory system prevents customer dissatisfaction and cuts down on handling expenses for your business. Furthermore, it allows you to anticipate how much stock will be needed in the future so you can plan ahead accordingly.

Inventory systems can be costly to implement, but they pay off in the long run. Neglecting inventory management could result in lost sales, disruptions to production or customer service operations, as well as lower profits overall.

Working Capital Statements and Financial Ratios

Working capital statements and financial ratios provide insight into your company's cash flow position and performance. They offer an overview of where your company stands currently, enabling you to determine how much capital is available for future operations.

The working capital ratio is an important indicator of liquidity, as it shows your capacity to pay off debts. A healthy ratio ranges between 1.2 and 2.0 depending on the industry in which you operate.

A positive working capital ratio indicates you have more cash available than what you owe, signaling to lenders and investors that you are responsible for servicing your debts. Conversely, a negative working capital ratio implies you owe more than what is owed - an indication that your business needs to increase its cash flow.

Fund and cash flow statements

Fund and cash flow statements are essential financial tools that enable you to monitor your business's cash flow and performance. They enable you to recognize trends in your cash flows and effectively manage them.

A company requires sufficient positive cash flow to run its operations and pay employees, suppliers and vendors. Furthermore, it needs sufficient liquidity to cover short-term expenses and investments.

Maintaining a company's cash flow on an ongoing basis is essential for staying solvent and avoiding having to borrow funds for operations. This can be accomplished through routine analysis of the company's cash flow statements and other financial records.

Overhead

Overhead refers to all expenses related to running your business that aren't directly associated with producing goods or services. This includes office supplies, rent, utilities and salaries for administrative staff members. Overhead is an essential metric for tracking cash flow and financial performance. It helps ensure costs are kept low, prices remain competitive, and revenues are maximized.

C. Understanding and managing tax obligations

No matter if you file your taxes yourself or seek professional assistance, it is essential to comprehend and manage your tax responsibilities. By taking advantage of available adjustments, deductions and credits, you can reduce the size of your tax bill while keeping more of what you earn.

One of the best ways to save for retirement is by taking advantage of your retirement savings plans. These accounts automatically deduct from your paycheck, making saving for retirement much simpler and efficient.

Maximize your retirement savings plans

Understanding and managing your tax obligations can make a substantial impact on the quality of life in retirement, particularly with regard to Social Security and Medicare benefits. To maximize your savings, begin early, save diligently and increase contributions gradually over time. Aim to save at least 15% of your salary annually.

If you're self-employed or own a small business, SEP IRAs are an excellent way to save for retirement. With this plan, you can contribute up to 20% of your net income which could provide an impressive boost in retirement funds.

Use your employee benefits

Employee benefits refer to any non-cash compensation paid to an employee in addition to their salary. These could include health insurance or financial planning assistance, but the primary aim is always the same: helping employees feel satisfied and invested in their job.

In fact, these programs can actually enhance employee productivity and retention by helping them better manage their own wellbeing. Selecting an employee benefits package that provides your employees with a beneficial package without breaking the bank can take some careful consideration and analysis. Start by understanding which benefits are legally mandated and how much it costs to provide them.

Pay the right amount

One of the greatest challenges businesses face is understanding and managing tax obligations. This includes federal taxes such as income, sales and payroll taxes; state and local taxes like excise taxes or property taxes; both can be quite onerous to comprehend and manage effectively.

Paying taxes on time is of the utmost importance. If you fail to make a payment, the IRS will charge 4% interest and a penalty of 1/2 percent per month, up to 25% of your outstanding balance each year.

Make the most of your adjustments

Tax bills can be a real pain in the neck, but if you're fortunate enough to receive one, the burden can be eased with some forward planning and adjustments to your income taxes. Review all your documents carefully to ensure all deductions and benefits are claimed correctly. Then read through our list of helpful tidbits that could save you money when the taxman calls. You might be amazed at how much money can be saved with smart financial management - like diverting up to $19,500 from your paycheck into a 401(k) without being taxed?

Deductions and credits

Deductions and credits can be a huge money saver if you know how to claim them. Unfortunately, they're also complex to understand, so it's wise to consult an accountant or tax professional for assistance in figuring out which deductions are worth claiming. Tax deductions reduce taxable income for individuals by decreasing the amount of income tax they owe. However, the value of a deduction depends on the taxpayer's marginal tax rate, which increases with income.

File on time

Taxes can be a hassle and many people attempt to avoid them. But filing on time is essential if you want to minimize penalties.

In addition to filing early, ensure all necessary documents are prepared when starting to work on your return. These include W-2 or 1099 forms, any income statements and documents related to stocks, pensions or trust funds. If you miss the tax filing and payment deadlines due to illness or a fire, many times penalty charges can be avoided. This is especially true if there was an unforeseen calamity such as serious illness.

D. Using financial tools and software

Financial tools and software are essential elements of financial management for any business. They enable you to monitor cash flow income and expenditure, providing insight into your company's overall health. The right tools can save you time and money in other areas of your business. They enable budget management, asset analysis, and more.

Tracking Cash Flow Income and Outgoings

There are a range of financial tools and software programs available to help you keep tabs on your cash flow income and outgoings. Some are free, while others require a nominal charge.

Google Sheets, for instance, is a popular free option that enables users to create and save cash flow statements. It's easy to share these documents with others and works across computers and mobile devices alike. Cashflow tracking software can be extremely beneficial in managing cash flows over a period of time and is customizable for any situation or business type.

Another popular option is QuickBooks, which features a cash-flow forecast feature. This can assist businesses in estimating how much money they'll need for operating expenses during any given period.

These tools make budgeting much simpler. They enable you to set achievable savings goals based on your income and expense data, plus they have visual tools that encourage progress monitoring and motivation.

Keeping an Eye on Your Financial Health

Financial tools and software can be an excellent way to stay on top of your finances and make informed decisions. These programs enable you to monitor income and expenses, create budgets, and pay bills with ease.

Small businesses and startups can benefit from using these tools to ensure their financial health. There are various tools available for tracking income and expenses, so make sure you select one that works best for you. Mint is an app designed to keep tabs on all of your finances in one place. It automatically pulls credit card and bank transactions, categorizes them, and displays how you spend money. Furthermore, Mint provides access to your credit score as well as insight into how well you're managing debt.

Managing Budgets and Cash Flows

Utilizing financial tools and software to manage your budgets can help you stay on top of spending, savings, and cash flow. This is especially useful if you're working towards building an emergency fund.

A budget is a detailed plan of how you intend to use your money over an extended period. It differs from a cash flow statement in that it includes both income and outgoings for multiple months at once.

Budgeting software typically provides features that simplify many daily accounting tasks for small businesses. This could include automation of payments, automatic billing and past-due notifications - saving both business owners and their employees a lot of time in the process.

Keeping Track of Assets

Tracking assets means identifying and tracking the location, condition and maintenance of equipment, machinery, vehicles, tools and other vital resources. Asset tracking systems are essential for companies to guarantee their assets remain in optimal condition while helping businesses boost their profitability.

Asset management software solutions enable companies to easily tag, sort, and keep records of their assets. These programs often utilize barcodes, serial numbers, and QR codes as unique identifiers in order to guarantee accurate tracking of information. Tracking systems for assets can help businesses reduce the cost of asset loss and prevent theft. They give managers and employees valuable insights into an asset's status, maintenance schedule, and ownership.

E. Seeking professional financial advice and guidance

Seeking professional financial advice and guidance can be an excellent way to stay on track with your finances. Additionally, it may give you greater assurance and peace of mind regarding your money management decisions.

When searching for a financial advisor, it's essential to do your due diligence and research the available options. Once you know what you require from an advisor, then you can focus on narrowing down your search by identifying what it is that you require.

What to Look for

If you're in the process of purchasing or selling a home, planning for retirement, saving for college or dealing with any major life change, seeking professional financial advice and guidance can be an advantageous step.

The initial step is to decide which financial advisor is suitable for you. Doing this requires asking them questions about their qualifications and how they get paid, so that you can make an informed decision regarding whether their services are beneficial to your circumstances. You should also look for an advisor who is willing to explain their work in detail. They should explain why they recommend a particular investment, if they receive commission on certain transactions and any potential conflicts of interest they may have.

Find a Real Fiduciary

When seeking professional financial advice and guidance, look for an advisor who is a fiduciary. This means they must put their clients' interests before their own, disclose any conflicts of interest and avoid selling products that do not support your goals.

Finding a qualified fiduciary is simple; ask those you trust for their recommendations. Most likely, they will have experience and insight into which advisors they recommend.

Check Their Credentials

Verifying an individual's credentials typically involves checking with their state government office. This includes verifying the education and employment history of teachers, contractors and other professionals such as medical practitioners and tax experts.

When seeking a financial advisor, it's essential to look for someone with an appropriate professional designation such as CFA or CFP. This demonstrates they have acquired extensive knowledge and passed rigorous exams. Furthermore, these individuals agree to uphold a code of ethics.

Understand How They Get Paid

When seeking professional financial advice and guidance, understanding how an advisor gets paid can make all the difference in how they work with you. A reliable advisor should put your needs ahead of their own financial gain while keeping you informed throughout every step of the process.

They typically generate income by charging clients fees for investment management or financial planning services. These may include percentage-based management fees as well as flat or hourly financial planning rates.

Look for Fee-Only Advisors

You can search for fee-only advisors online or through a local association. Organizations that specialize in this area include NAPFA, XY

Planning Network, and The Garrett Planning Network. Finding an advisor who meets your needs and is a good fit for you is key. Look for a fiduciary or financial planner with appropriate credentials and professional experience so they can make knowledgeable recommendations.

If you're searching for a fee-only investment advisor, make sure they are members of NAPFA (National Association of Personal Financial Advisors). These individuals cannot accept commissions or fees from insurance companies or product providers.

Search for Clarity

Finding the ideal financial adviser or CPA can make a world of difference in your life and career. Whether you're buying your first home or trying to pay off debt, having an understanding of where you stand financially and what can be done with it is key. A sound financial plan combined with smart savings strategies will put you on the road to prosperity. Additionally, consult with them regularly throughout life - even for something as simple as creating a budget or setting goals and timelines for yourself and your family.

Find an Advisor Who Keeps You On Track

Financial advisors are like life coaches for your money. They help you manage and rebalance your portfolio, suggest specific products, and steer you away from risky investments to ensure that you stay on track to reach your financial objectives.

They can assist in managing your debt and creating a budget to save for the things you desire in life, like buying a home or paying off college.

Finding the ideal professional can be daunting, but it is an essential step in reaching your objectives. To find a suitable advisor, ask family and friends for recommendations or utilize a free matching service offered by professional matchmakers.

Conclusion

In sum, launching a company is a thrilling and perilous adventure. In any case, having access to insider information may improve the likelihood of a good outcome. This book provides 50 helpful hints for launching a business, covering everything from creating a business strategy and performing market research to selecting a company name, as well as establishing and maintaining positive connections, making use of technology, and striving for constant improvement. If you follow these guidelines, you'll give your company the best chance of being sustainable in the long run by allowing it to change and grow with the times.

The need of always being open to change is stressed throughout the text. Businesses that are nimble enough to adjust to new circumstances rapidly have a better chance of thriving. This requires you to be flexible, to try new things, to take calculated chances, and to keep learning. You must also be ready to assess the performance of your pricing plan and make adjustments as required.

Making solid connections is crucial when first starting out in a company. Among them include fostering connections with supply-chain partners, forming partnerships with competitors, and providing incentives to staff. Building reliable relationships with like-minded people allows you to connect with a network of people who care about your development and success.

One of the most crucial elements of launching a company is establishing a variety of payment methods. Customers are more likely to do business with you again if you make it simple for them to pay you. You may do this by providing a variety of payment options (such as PayPal, credit cards, and more).

Finally, never stop trying to become better and educate yourself. Improve your offerings on a regular basis by encouraging creativity, promoting openness in communication, and making use of feedback from your customers.

Provide outstanding customer service even after the deal is made, and seek out new ways to improve.

In conclusion, launching a company isn't easy, but it's also not impossible. If you follow the advice in this book, you'll be able to establish a solid foundation for your firm and make it more flexible as time goes on. If you can keep your mind on the task at hand, have a positive outlook, and never stop seeking knowledge, you will have a great foundation upon which to develop a successful enterprise.